The GIFT *of* GOD's WORD

PAMELLA CHRISTENSEN

The Gift of God's Word

Executive Press Ltd
Edmonton AB T6A 0H7
Canada
343-554-1210

The views expressed in this work are solely those of the author and do not necessarily reflect the views of the publisher, and the publisher hereby disclaims any responsibility for them.

Any people depicted in stock imagery provided by Getty Images are models, and such images are being used for illustrative purposes only.
Certain stock imagery © Getty Images.

THE HOLY BIBLE, NEW INTERNATIONAL VERSION®, NIV® Copyright © 1973, 1978, 1984, 2011 by Biblica, Inc.® Used by permission. All rights reserved worldwide.

Scripture taken from the New King James Version®. Copyright © 1982 by Thomas Nelson. Used by permission. All rights reserved.

The Living Bible copyright © 1971 by Tyndale House Foundation. Used by permission of Tyndale House Publishers Inc., Carol Stream, Illinois 60188. All rights reserved. The Living Bible, TLB, and the The Living Bible logo are registered trademarks of Tyndale House Publishers.

[Scripture quotations are]from the Revised Standard Version of the Bible, copyright © 1946, 1952, and 1971 the Division of Christian Education of the National Council of the Churches of Christ in the United States of America. Used by permission. All rights reserved.

Paperback ISBN: 979-8-9913174-2-9
Hardcover ISBN: 979-8-9913174-3-6

Library of Congress Control Number: 2021908471

The of Gift of God's Word

Contents

In the Beginning—The First Seven Days 7

Genesis: In the Beginning—The First Seven Days.................... 9

Genesis: In the Beginning—The First Seven Days.................13

Genesis: In the Beginning— The First Seven Days 16

Genesis: In the Beginning—The First Seven Days.................20

Genesis: In the Beginning—The First Seven Days.................23

Genesis: In the Beginning—The First Seven Days.................27

Genesis: In the Beginning—The First Seven Days.................30

Genesis: In the Beginning—The First Seven Days.................33

Genesis: In the Beginning—The First Seven Days.................36

Introducing Old and New Testament Verses and Devotions.40

Our Heavenly Father's Redeeming Love 42

A Sad Story with a Happy Ending 44

God's Wonderful Promises........................46

Music Is a Glorious Gift from God! 48

Knowing God Personally 50

Almighty God, Please Give Me the Strength!........................52

We Must Confess Our Sins........................54

Naaman Healed of Leprosy / A Little Child Shall Lead Them........................56

From Fear to Honor........................58

"All Things Have Become New!" 60

The Blessing of Self-Control 62

The Guiding Star..64

Herod's Terrible Plan..66

Looking Ahead to the Kingdom of Heaven................68

The Power of Peace 70

Lord, I Want to Be a Tree 72

Meeting God on the Mountaintop.............................74

I Am Jesus's Little Lamb..76

Hosanna! 78

Follow the Father's Will..80

Where Is Judas?...82

The New Covenant...84

Netting a Prize Catch..85

And That's the Truth! 86

Topsy-Turvy..88

Always Be Ready!...90

The Death of Two Thieves...92

A Very Personal Bible Study 94

"Go and Sin No More!"...96

The Fall of the Evil Prince 98

What Is Jesus Saying?.. 100

Blood and Water 102

All in His Time.. 105

An Amazingly Wonderful Body Part.......................... 107

Sitting with My Heavenly Dad 109

Gratitude for Those Who Prayed for and Witnessed to My

Soul.. 111

Worry-Free! 113

For Yours is the Kingdom and the Power and the Glory

Forever! Amen. 115

This poem is based on both Old and New Testament Bible

stories.. 118

On a Pathway through Some Psalms............................... 120

On a Pathway through Some Psalms 122

On a Pathway through Some Psalms: *Psalm 23—A Psalm of*

David.. 124

On a Pathway through Some Psalms: *Psalm 40—A Christlike*

Attitude.. 127

On a Pathway through Some Psalms: *What Gift Can I Possibly*

Give?... 132

On a Pathway through Some Psalms: *Psalms 78 and 116—*

Giving Thanks!.. 134

On a Pathway through Some Psalms: *Psalm 119 #1—Praise to*

the Word of God 139

On a Pathway through Some Psalms: *Psalm 119 #2—Praise*

tothe Word of God!...142

On a Pathway through Some Psalms: *Psalm 150—Praise and*

Worship...146

On a Pathway through Some Psalms Conclusion 148

A Poetic Reflection Based on Bible Verses 149

Pam Talks to Parents 151

Pam Talks to Parents 153

Pam Talks to Parents: September 155

Pam Talks to Parents: October 157

Pam Talks to Parents: November 158

Pam Talks to Parents: December 159

Pam Talks to Parents: January 160

Pam Talks to Parents: February 162

Pam Talks to Parents: March 163

Pam Talks to Parents: April 165

Pam Talks to Parents: May 166

Pam Talks to Parents: June 168

Pam Talks to Parents: July 169

Pam Talks to Parents: August 171

Some Concluding Thoughts on The Gift of God's Word 173

The Holy Bible is a wonderful book that shares with us many stories, all being the true Word of God.

As I studied both the Old and New Testaments, I also led Bible studies for forty-nine years, and God inspired me to write quite a few of them, which I then shared with many people.

This book begins with a study from the book of Genesis: "In the Beginning—The First Seven Days."

The second portion of the book is a selection of Bible verses and devotions based on both "Old and New Testament Verses, from Genesis to Revelation."

The third section will lead you "On a Pathway through Some Psalms."

The fourth and final section confronts the challenges of raising children throughout the year:
"Pam Talks to Parents."

Many of the Bible verses that are referred to come from the New King James Version (NKJV). But other translations are also used, including the Concordia Self-Study Bible; the Lutheran Study Bible (LSB); the New International Version (NIV); The Living Bible (TLB); and the Revised Standard Version (RSV).

I hope and pray that all four sections of this book will bring you joy as you grow closer to God through the study of His Word!

My heart is stirred by a noble theme
as I recite my verses for the king;
my tongue is the pen of a skillful writer.
(Psalm 45:1 NIV)

Gifts are fun to receive and fun to give.

Some gifts are surprises; others we know about.

The Bible offers comments about gifts. One is found in James 1:17 (NKJV):

Every good and perfect gift is from above, and comes down from the Father of lights, with Whom there is no shadow of turning.

God doesn't change. We can count on Him. He doesn't ever take back the gifts He has given to us.
Romans 8:32 (NKJV) speaks of this:

He Who did not spare His own Son, but delivered Him up for us all, how shall He not with Him also freely give us all things?

It's exciting to realize how much God loves us and that He has a bounty of gifts to bestow on us.

What can some of these gifts be? Write down some of the gifts God has given to you.

Here is what Psalm 37:4 (NKJV) tells us:

Delight yourself also in the Lord, and He shall give you the desires of your heart.

I absolutely love this promise of God! This verse doesn't mean that God will give me everything my heart desires. Instead, it means that He will put the right desires—His desires—into my heart. Then, when I pray, I can be assured that I am praying according to God's will.

First John 5:14–15 (NKJV) declares:

Now this is the confidence that we have in Him, that if we ask anything according to His will, He hears us. And if we know that He hears us, whatever we ask, we know that we have the petitions that we have asked of Him.

Have you ever had the experience of praying for something according to God's will? How did things turn out? If you are willing, share your experience with others.

In addition to the desires of our hearts, what else will God give to us? He gives us, as Martin Luther said, all that I need to support this body and life. Jesus taught us to ask God to supply these needs and to trust His provision when He taught us to pray, "Give us this day our daily bread" (Matthew 6:11 NKJV).

God not only provides us with daily bread; He also gives us Living Water. Listen to what Jesus said to the Samaritan woman as recorded in John 4:10 (NKJV):

"If you knew the gift of God, and Who it is Who says to you, 'Give Me a drink,' you would have asked Him, and He would have given you Living Water."

Of course, Jesus's words are for us as well, and the gift of Living Water is available to each of us. But what exactly does this Living Water mean for us? The answer is found in Romans 6:23 (NKJV):

For the wages of sin is death, but the gift of God is eternal life in Christ Jesus our Lord.

And Ephesians 2:8 (NKJV) says this:

By grace you have been saved, through faith, and that not of yourselves; it is the gift of God.

God has also given us individual gifts, unique to each of our personalities. First Corinthians 7:7 (NKJV) tells us this:

Each one has his or her own gift from God, one in this manner and another in that.

First Corinthians 12:4 calls this a "diversity of gifts." Do you recognize a diversity of gifts among other members of your family, friends, and church members?

What are we to do with the gifts we receive from God? First, we are to meditate on what God has given us and then give ourselves entirely to learning to *use* our gifts, according to 1 Timothy 4:15, so that our progress in our Christian walk may be evident to all.

Then, as we do good to those around us, we will become rich in good works, ready to give, willing to share, not only to be a blessing to those around us but also to store up for ourselves a good foundation for the times to come, that we may lay hold on eternal life (1 Timothy 6:18–19).

Just before Jesus left this world, He gave all of us a new commandment. His words are recorded in John 13:34–35 (NKJV):

"A new commandment I give to you, that you love one another, as I have loved you; that you also love one another. By this all will know that you are My disciples, if you have love for one another."

This wonderful love is a precious gift from Jesus, who is God, who is love. This gift allows each of us to reflect the love of Jesus to the world around us, a world that is so black with sin and yet can be made bright with this reflected love.

What can we give back to the Lord?

Second Thessalonians 2:13 (NKJV) sums this up well: "We are bound to give thanks to God always!"

The Holy Bible, a wonderful gift from God that He inspired many authors to write, over many centuries, tells us everything we need to know about the Triune God: our wonderful heavenly Father, the Creator of the world; Jesus, His Son, who came to earth as a person to save us from our sins; and the Holy Spirit, who inspires us with our faith.

Martin Rinckart, who lived from 1586 to 1694, wrote a famous hymn that expresses our thanks for the many and wonderful gifts that God gives to us. Here are verses 1 and 3 from that hymn:

> Now thank we all our God, with heart and hands and voices,
> Who wondrous things has done, in Whom this world rejoices;
> Who from our mother's arms has blessed us on our way
> With countless gifts of love, and still is ours today.

All praise and thanks to God the Father now be given,
The Son, and Him Who reigns with Them in highest heaven—
The one Eternal God, Whom earth and heaven adore!
For thus it was, is now, and shall be evermore!

In the Beginning—The First Seven Days

Before creation ever came to be,
Jehovah—three in one and one in three—
Already had a special place for me.

Before the birth of matter, time and space,
God knew me. Then, by His almighty grace,
My life was given substance, time, and place.

With joy and love and great anticipation,
God first prepared a gift, His own creation;
A perfect home for men of every nation.

Over the restless waters, dark as night,
God's Spirit hovered. Then, His voice of might
And mystery proclaimed, "Let there be light!"

That eve and morn together were day one.
Yet the Creator's work was far from done.
The world in which I live had just begun!

Between the waters low and heavens high,
God next created atmosphere, so I
Would not be crushed by His created sky.

With day two now complete, God's declaration
Was that the earth should strive with vegetation.
How lush and green the third day of creation!

The fourth day's focus went up very high
As sun and moon and stars filled the dark sky—
A compass on which travelers could rely!

On the fifth day, the earth became alive
With music! Color! Motion! Birds did thrive,
Sing, swoop, and fly! And fish did leap and dive!

On day six, a cacophony of sound
Now filled the earth, as over all the ground,
Beasts large and small, both tame and wild, were found.

But God had more to do on that sixth day:
He formed a man from His created clay,
Then breathed into the man His breath of life!
(From that man's rib God also made a wife.)

Inspired by Genesis chapter 1.

Genesis: In the Beginning— The First Seven Days

The quoted verses in these nine lessons are all from the New King James Version (NKJV).

Lesson 1—Introduction

Opening Prayer

Dear LORD God, my loving Heavenly Father,

As I look into Your Word today and begin this study of the creation of the world, I ask that through Your Holy Spirit You would be my teacher. Help me to surrender my mind to You. Help me to think clearly, to seek Your truth, and to grow in my faith. I come to You boldly with these requests, in the name of Jesus. Amen.

Introduction

Genesis 1:2 states that prior to the creation story, there was an empty, formless void, and the eternal Spirit of God hovered over deep waters. These are symbols of chaos and evil, into which God stepped to create order and goodness. All of the angels, both good and bad, preexisted the creation of the world. Satan, known as Lucifer, began as one of the highest angels (see Ezekiel 28:12–17), but he rebelled against God and was cast out (see Isaiah 14:12–15). The Bible sometimes refers to angels as stars. Prior to his fall, Lucifer, Satan, was sometimes called "the star of the morning." When Satan fell from God, he took one-third of the angels with him (see Revelation 12:4). The story of creation as revealed in Genesis chapter 1 begins with the creation of time and light, and the separation of good from evil, with everything good created simply by God's Word.

1. Goals of this study

A. Understand each day of creation.
B. Examine creation versus evolution and see why it matters.
C. Grow in faith.

2. Introduction

Genesis, a book of beginnings, was written by Moses, who wrote the first five books of the Bible, known as the Pentateuch. The first eleven chapters discuss the origins of the world. Chapters 12–50 present the origins of the people of Israel, specifically Abraham and his descendants.

Moses is the author of Genesis, but God told him what to write:

A. Read 2 Timothy 3:16a.
B. Read 2 Peter 1:21.

3. The beginning: read Genesis 1:1–2

God wants the truth of His creation story to be told. What does God say about the teaching of evolution?

A. Read Romans 1:18–22.
B. Read also Romans 1:28–32.
C. The Bible speaks of God's preexistence to the world. Read Psalm 90:2.

4. "In the beginning ..."

A. These words indicate the creation of time. Read Psalm 102:25.

B. Jesus Christ is God's Wisdom. Read Wisdom's story in Proverbs 8:22–31.

5. "God ..."

A. God is a Trinity. Read the first part of Genesis 1:26.

B. The book of James describes God the Father as perfect. Read James 1:13 and 17.

C. God the Son, Jesus, is described as "the Word" in John 1:1–3. Also read Psalm 33:6.

D. Read a further description of the God the Son in Colossians 1:15–17.

E. Hebrews 1:2–3 also attests to the fact that Jesus, a person of the Trinity, is the Creator.

F. God is also a Spirit, as referred to in Genesis 1:2. This third person of the Triune God is mentioned in many other places throughout the Bible. All three persons of the Trinity, as mentioned in Genesis 1:26, were present at Jesus's baptism. Read Matthew 3:16–17.

G. What does Psalm 14:1 have to say about people who scoff at the notion of a creator God?

6. "Created the heavens (space) and the earth (matter)"

Both the Old and New Testaments have comments about this aspect of creation.

A. Read Isaiah 66:1–2, and then for further comment from God, read Isaiah 55:9.

B. Colossians 1:15–19 speaks of the supremacy of Christ in creation. Read those verses.

C. How can we comprehend the creation story? Read Hebrews 11:3.

Closing Prayer

Dear LORD, Creator of all, please create in me a new heart, a heart that will love You above everything else. Create in me the faith that I need to believe that You lovingly made each of us individually and uniquely and with an eternal purpose. Finally, LORD, create in my heart the desire to share what I know of you with the world around me. In Jesus's name I pray. Amen.

Genesis: In the Beginning—
The First Seven Days

Lesson 2—The First Day

Opening Prayer

Dear LORD God, my loving Heavenly Father,

It is so exciting to look into Your Word! Through Your Holy Spirit, You reveal new truths to me each time I read the Bible because it is Your *living* Word. Help me learn something new about you today that will defend me from the darkness of unbelief and will strengthen me with the light of faith.

I ask this in the name of your Son, Jesus. Amen.

    1. The Lutheran Study Bible offers this description of the title *Genesis*:

The first phrase of the Hebrew text of 1:1 is *bereshith* ("in the beginning"), which is also the Hebrew title of the book (books in ancient times customarily were named after their first word or two). The English title, *Genesis*, is Greek in origin and comes from the word that appears in the Greek translation (Septuagint) of 2:4 and 5:1. Depending on its context, the word can mean "birth," "genealogy," or "history of origin." In both its Hebrew and Greek forms, the title of Genesis appropriately describes its contents, since it is primarily a "book of beginnings."

A. Read Genesis 1:1–2. Jeremiah quotes the concept of the earth being "formless and empty" in Jeremiah 4:23. It is the only other biblical reference to this concept. In it, Jeremiah envisions his land in ruins and compares this sorrow to a reversal of creation. Read that verse.

B. How long did it take for the earth and universe as we know it to come about? This is a huge area of debate in our time. Do we accept the theory of evolution, or do we accept God's revealed Word as truth? Read what God reveals in Exodus 20:11.

C. When the Bible introduces God in Genesis 1:1, His existence is fully assumed. Although everything created had a beginning, God Himself existed from eternity. Read Psalm 90:2.

2. "The Spirit of God" hovered over the formless, empty darkness. God in the original Hebrew is *Elohim*, a word that describes the majesty of the one true God. Read Genesis 2:7, which uses that same word again.

A. God's Sprit was "hovering over the waters," the symbol of evil and chaos over which God hovered with His awesome, light-giving, order-making, life-creating Word. The Bible offers other references with the word "hover." Read Deuteronomy 32:10–11, which describes God's protection of Jacob. Read also Isaiah 31:5.

B. Another reference to Genesis1:1 appears in 2 Peter 3:3–7. Read those verses.

3. Read Genesis 1:3. "And God said ..." God brought all things into being merely by speaking. Read other references in Psalm 33:6–9, Psalm 148:5, and Hebrews 11:3.

A. In the Old Testament, there are many references that describe light as a symbol of life and blessing. Read 2 Samuel 22:29, Psalm 56:13, Psalm 97:11, and Psalm 119:105 for examples. In the New Testament, Paul refers to light to illustrate God's recreating work in hearts darkened by sin. Read 2 Corinthians 4:6.

B. Not only did God create light, but He *is* the light. Read Luke 2:25–32 (especially verse 32), John 8:12, 2 Corinthians 4:4, and 1 John 1:5.

C. And "the light was good." Read verses 10, 12, 17–18, 25, and 31a from Genesis 1.

D. "He separated the light from the darkness." Read Psalm 104:20–23 and Psalm 127:2.

E. "God called ..." Read Psalm 74:16. (Everything belongs to God, who named what He created.)

F. "The evening and the morning were the first day." Read Genesis 1:5, 1:8, 13, 19, 23, and 31.

G. Were these literal days or figurative days? Some people refer to Psalm 90:4 to say that the days of creation may have each lasted for a long, long time. Such an interpretation then leaves room for things on earth to evolve. Second Peter 3:8 says the same thing but then goes on, in verse 9, to explain that this relates to God's patience with bringing the final judgment to the world. The Bible uses the words "evening" and "morning" in other places to say that the six-day work week was established by God. Read, for example, Genesis 2:3 and Exodus 20:9–11.

Closing Prayer

Dear Lord God, Creator of all,

Today I have taken a closer look at the very first days of creation, the beginning of time, the beginning of history. Please guide me with the light of Your love as I walk with You through the week ahead. Illumine my heart so that I can accept by faith what I am unable to explain or understand. Be my light, Lord. Help me to think of You with praise in my heart when I rise in the morning and relax in the evening.

In Jesus's name. Amen.

Genesis: In the Beginning—
The First Seven Days

Lesson 3—The Second Day

Opening Prayer

Dear Father in heaven,

As I continue my study of the world's first seven days, fill me with awe and wonder.

As I think of how You made the world, teach me to say with Paul, "O the depth of the riches both of the wisdom and knowledge of God!" (Romans 11:33 NKJV) Please be my teacher, Lord. Amen.

    1. What was created on the second day? Read Genesis 1:6–8. The "sky" that is described is the atmosphere as seen from the earth, from our point of view. Read Job 37:18 and Isaiah 40:12 for other biblical pictorial descriptions of the "sky."

And God said, "Let there be an expanse between the waters to separate water from water." (NIV)

    2. Later in the Bible, God says that He is the one who stretched out the heavens. Read Isaiah 44:24.

The first reference to this division of waters in the history of humanity is found in the story of Noah, recorded in Genesis 7:11–12 and in 8:1–3. Read those verses. It appears that there had never been any rain until God opened the heavens, after first closing the door on the ark to protect Noah, his wife, his three sons, and their wives from the oncoming forty days of rain. God had allowed Noah one hundred years to construct the ark and witness to God's approaching judgment. Following the forty days of rain, which—combined with water that gushed up from inside the earth—covered everything on earth, Noah, his family, and all of the animals spent a full year floating on the water before it receded and they were able to leave the ark. All of this is an amazing study of its own!

3. Other references to this early aspect of creation pertain to God's provision for His people (read Psalm 78:12–16); His promise of blessing (read Malachi 3:10); and Isaiah's prediction of salvation from God (read Isaiah 51:10).

"And it was so" (Genesis 1:7 KJV). This is the only possible outcome to God's spoken Word.

4. "And God called the expanse sky" (Genesis 1:8 KJV).

God is the one who controls the sky, as He tells Job in Job 37:14–16.

David commented on the sky in Psalm 19:1.

Psalm 104:1–13 comments on both the sky and the waters that were separated by God.

Isaiah 40:21–22 gives us a visual description of where to find God.

Jeremiah 10:11–13 speaks of this aspect of creation to compare the true Creator God to pagan idols.

There was evening and there was morning—the second day. (Genesis 1:8 KJV)

5. "Theistic evolution" is the hybrid notion that the creation story is not factual and that God was somehow involved in the process of evolution. Why is this a problem? Because if the account of creation is only partially true, then the fall of humankind may not have been an actual event; and if that is true, there is no need for a Savior because humans have the ability to work out their own problems. We need to accept the total story of creation as told in the scriptures, or else the revelations about Jesus as the Messiah, our only hope of salvation, are unimportant and unneeded.

6. What does the Bible say about Jesus in the creation story?

In 1 Corinthians 1:24, Jesus Christ is presented as equal to God. Read 1 Corinthians 1:23–24.

In the Old Testament, Jesus, the Messiah, is revealed to be a part of the creation story. Read Proverbs 8:22–31.

In John 1:1–4, Jesus, referred to as the Word, is again revealed to have been the Creator.

Paul speaks about faith in God as a gift of the Spirit. Read 2 Corinthians 1:19–22. If we have accepted by faith that the creation story, as presented in the Bible, is true, we have not reached that conclusion on our own. No, that faith is a gift of the Holy Spirit. Our response is to share that faith when conversations about evolution arise.

No one can refute our own experiences and testimonies. Whether others agree with us or not, our witness gives them something to ponder, and we can pray that the Holy Spirit will also guide them to accept the truths of the Bible.

Closing Prayer

Dear God,

Thank You for revealing Yourself to me through Your Word. Give me the desire to learn more about You so that I will never waver in my faith and I will always be willing to share that faith with others. I ask this in the name of Your Son, Jesus. Amen.

Genesis: In the Beginning— The First Seven Days

Lesson 4—The Third Day

Opening Prayer

Praise befits You, O God! I am filled with the good things of Your house. You formed the mountains by Your power. Where morning dawns and evening fades, You call them forth with songs of joy. You care for the land, and You water it; You enrich it abundantly and provide Your people with grain. You crown the earth with Your bounty. The grasslands of the desert overflow; the hills are clothed with gladness. The valleys are mantled with grain; they shout for joy and sing. O God, please fill me, too, with joy over Your beautiful world! Amen.

1. Read about the third day of Creation in Genesis 1:9–13.

The opening prayer was inspired by verses found in Psalm 65. Read verses 8–13.

Psalm 104 is another commentary about God's creation. Read verses 5–28.

First Corinthians 15:37–38 speaks of the "seed-bearing plants and trees" that God created. Read those verses.

2. Other passages in Genesis comment about various life forms reproducing "according to their various kinds."

Read Genesis 1:12, 21, 24, and 25. Then read Genesis 6:19–20 and Genesis 7:14–15 from the story of Noah.

3. The Bible has comments about the resurrected body and its form. In the Old Testament, read Daniel 12:2–3. Then from the New Testament, read 1 Corinthians 15:39n44. Jesus speaks of this in John 12:23–25.

There are some interesting comparisons between Old Testament and New Testament verses on this topic.

Look again at 1 Corinthians 15. Compare verse 46 with Psalm 90:3. Compare verse 47 with John 3:13 and 31.

Compare verse 48 with Philippians 3:20–21. Finally, compare verse 49 with Genesis 5:3 and Romans 8:29–30.

4. How are we, as Christians, to live in this world? Read the parable of the weeds in Matthew 13:24–29. Then read Jesus's explanation of His parable in Matthew 13:36–43.

5. How can we, as Christians, examine our hearts? Read first Jesus's parable of the sower in Matthew 13:3–9.

Then read His explanation of the parable in Matthew 13:18–23.

Finally, how should we, as Christians, respond to the harvest? Read Matthew 9:37–38.

Closing Prayer

LORD, as I examine day three of Your creation week, I am led to proclaim with the psalmist, "Come and see what God has done; how awesome are His works in man's behalf!" (Psalm 66:5 NIV). You created all that grows for our aesthetic pleasure, for our nourishment, and for giving us a picture of the kingdom of heaven. Now use me, LORD, to help me spread Your good news to those who are near to me and to the ends of the earth. In the name of Your Son, Jesus, I pray. Amen.

Genesis: In the Beginning—
The First Seven Days

Lesson 5—The Fourth Day

Opening Prayer

Read Psalm 136:1–9, 26 (NKJV). If you are with others, you may wish to read responsively.

O give thanks to the LORD, for He is good!
For His mercy endures forever.

O give thanks to the God of gods!
For His mercy endures forever!

O give thanks to the LORD of lords!
For His mercy endures forever.

To Him alone Who does great wonders:
For His mercy endures forever.

To Him Who by Wisdom made the heavens;
For His mercy endures forever.

To Him Who laid out the earth above the waters;
For His mercy endures forever.

To Him Who made great lights;
For His mercy endures forever.

The sun to rule by day;
For His mercy endures forever.

The moon and stars to rule by night;

For His mercy endures forever.

O give thanks to the God of heaven!
For His mercy endures forever!

1. Read about the fourth day of creation in Genesis 1:14–19.

God said, "Let there be lights in the expanse of the sky ..."

Read Psalm 74:16 (verse 17 is good also). Then reread Psalm 136:7–9.

"To separate the day from the night."

Read Genesis 1:4–5.

"And let them serve as signs to mark seasons and days and years" (NKJV).

Read Psalm 19:4b and 6. Also read Psalm 104:19.

2. Genesis 1:14–15 tells us why God created the heavenly lights. In other books of scripture, the LORD has comments about people's interpretations of the heavenly hosts that He created.

Read 2 Kings 17:14–16 and Deuteronomy 17:2–5.

"God made two great lights—the greater light ... and the lesser light" (NKJV).

Read Psalm 104:19–22; also read Jesus's comment in Matthew 5:45.

"He made the stars, also" (NKJV).

Read further comments from scripture about the heavenly hosts of stars that God created:

Nehemiah 9:6; Job 9:9; Job 38:1 and 31–33; Isaiah 40:26; and 1 Corinthians 15:41.

Read God's command for those who believe in His Son, Jesus, in Philippians 2:13–16a.

3. Reread Genesis 1:17–18. Notice that the lights were created by God to fulfill three different functions:

a) to give light to the earth; b) to govern the day and night; c) to separate light from darkness.

Two Old Testament references comment on this governing aspect.

Read Psalm 136:8–9 and Jeremiah 33:20 and 25a.

4. Will the created lights still govern in eternity?

Read Isaiah 60:19–20 and Revelation 21:22–25.

5. Angels are messengers of light. Hebrews chapter 1 speaks of the angels that God created.

Read verses 6–7 and verse 14.

When were the angels created? Had they already been created before the first day of creation that is recorded in Genesis chapter 1? Read Job 38:4–7.

The angels had most definitely been created before the seventh day. Read Genesis 2:1–2.

Closing Prayer

Dear LORD, our LORD,

When I consider Your heavens, the work of Your fingers, the moon and stars that You have set in place,

I can only exclaim, "How majestic is Your name in all the earth!" As the moon reflects the light of the sun to a dark night, help me to reflect Your Son to a world dark with sin. Keep me pure, LORD, and allow me to shine for You like a star in the universe. In Jesus's name, I praise You! Amen.

Genesis: In the Beginning—
The First Seven Days

Lesson 6—The Fifth Day

Opening Prayer

Dear Lord, my loving Creator God, I ask for Your blessing today as I consider the fifth day of creation and the marvelous way you filled the sky and seas with color, motion, and song. Thank You for giving us the dove as a symbol of Your Holy Spirit and the fish as a symbol of knowing Your Son. Please ready my heart to learn new truths about You as I study Your Word today. Amen.

1. Read Genesis 1:20–23. Then read a comment on this part of creation in Psalm 146:5–6 (especially verse 6).

2. The Bible declares that "God created the great creatures of the sea." They were complete and varied from the very beginning. This is quite opposite of the evolution theory. Read Psalm 148:7.

3. The Bible makes a number of references to a great sea monster called the Leviathan, an animal that no longer lives on the earth. (Perhaps it vanished at the time of the flood.) Read Psalm 74:13–14; Isaiah 27:1; and Ezekiel 32:2. According to the Bible, only God is strong enough to destroy the Leviathan, which may have represented Satan. Read Revelation 12:1–9.

4. The book of Job, which may be the oldest book of the Bible, has a number of references to this part of creation. Read

Job 3:8; 7:12; and all of Job chapter 41, which is God's own description of this amazing sea creature.

5. God created "every living and moving thing with which the water teems." Read further comment in Psalm 104:24–26.

6. God created "every winged bird according to its kind." This is restated in Genesis 2:19. Read that verse.

God Himself offers some comments about some of the birds that He created. (To me, some of this shows God's sense of humor!) Read Job 39:13–18 and then 39:26–30.

It is possible that this also includes the creation of insects. Read Deuteronomy 14:11–20.

The dove, one of the birds that God created, is a symbol of God's Holy Spirit. Read Genesis 7:24, Genesis 8:1, and Genesis 8:8–12. Then read Matthew 3:13–17.

7. The fish became a symbol of the Christian faith. Read Matthew 4:18–21, Mark 1:17, and Luke 5:1–11.

The Greek word ICTHYS means "fish." But the letters are the first letters of the Greek words meaning "Jesus Christ God's Son Savior." Ichthys (more commonly spelled Ichthus, or sometimes Ikhthus, from Greek: ἰχθύς, capitalized ΙΧΘΥΣ or ΙΧΘΥC) is the ancient and classical Greek word for "fish." In English, it refers to a symbol consisting of two intersecting arcs, the ends of the right side extending beyond the meeting point so as to resemble the profile of a fish. This design, used by early Christians as a secret symbol, is now known colloquially as the "sign of the fish" or the "Jesus fish."

Closing Prayer

O Lord, Your Word declares that Your thoughts are not our thoughts and Your ways are not our ways. I see such evidence of this in the great variety of Your creation. How could You conceive of all the birds, fish, insects, and the many ways they move, reproduce, and eat, and accomplish this all in one day? On this fifth day of creation, the mountains and hills burst into song before You! Please accept my praise too. Amen.

Genesis: In the Beginning— The First Seven Days

Lesson 7—The Sixth Day, Part I

Opening Prayer

Dear LORD, as I continue my study of the first seven days as revealed in the book of Genesis, open my heart and mind to learn more about You and grow in my faith and trust, through Your Holy Spirit. Amen.

1. Read Genesis 1:24–31. On this, the sixth day of creation, all of the land animals, both wild and domestic, were created; then God created human beings separately and differently and in His own image.

Unfortunately, many people put their focus on evolution rather than on God's creation; in fact, the theory of evolution is taught in many schools. If we truly believe that we evolved, rather than putting our trust in God's creation, there is no real meaning to our existence. This issue and controversy is truly one of the big debates of our present age. But when we believe what the Bible tells us, that we were created as creatures of God, each with an eternal destiny, this can illuminate our entire lives.

2. When they were first created, animals did not hunt and kill other animals for food. For that reason, Noah was able to take all sorts of birds and animals into the ark, where they lived together through the forty days and nights of rain and then for over two hundred more days before the water receded

enough for everyone to leave the ark. Read Genesis 7:13–17 and 24 and Genesis 8:1–19.

3. The first of earth's animals to be killed were sacrificed by God, their Creator. He used the animals' skins to make garments of covering for both Adam and Eve after they sinned. Read Genesis 3:21–24.

At some point after that, God described to His people the act of the sacrifice of animals to atone for sin. God's actual command is not spelled out in the scriptures, but the story of Adam and Eve's sons Cain and Abel illustrates that they already knew of God's directives concerning animal sacrifice. Read Genesis 4:1–7.

It may possibly be that in order to obtain an animal for sacrifice, Cain, who raised only crops, would have had to purchase an animal from his brother Abel or someone else who raised flocks. Cain's heart attitude did not reflect humility and sorrow for his sin. The Concordia Self-Study Bible comments that "God looked with favor on Abel and his offering because of Abel's faith" and further comments that "God did not look with favor on Cain and his offering," because Cain's "motivation and attitude were bad from the outset."

Other than being killed for sacrifice, animals were not killed to be eaten until after the flood. Extra pairs of clean animals and birds had been put into the ark to be designated for sacrifice (see Genesis 7:2–3 and 8:20).

Following that event, God gave people animals to eat (see Genesis 9:1–3).

4. The first specific mention of a lamb being used for sacrifice occurs in Genesis chapter 22. In this account of God's test of Abraham's faith, the command was that Abraham should sacrifice his son Isaac. (Abraham must have fully expected God to somehow raise Isaac from the dead, because God had promised Abraham that, through Isaac, the descendants of Abraham would become a great nation.) The discussion that Abraham and Isaac had concerning the lamb for the sacrifice indicates that God had given a command about using a lamb, even though that is not specifically found in the Bible before this event. Read Genesis 22:6–8.

As the story continued, an angel stopped Abraham from sacrificing Isaac, and God provided not a lamb but a ram for the sacrifice—possibly a strange animal to be found so high up on the mountain.

Later in the scriptures, specific directions were given by God concerning the lamb for sacrifice. It could be either from a sheep or a goat, a year-old male without defect. This is fully described in God's directions for the first Passover. Read Exodus 12:1–13.

The Passover lamb is a foreshadowing, or *type*, of Jesus, the sacrificial Lamb whose death paid for the sins of all people. Read John 1:29 and Revelation 5:6, 11–13.

Closing Prayer

Dear Lord,

From the very first week of creation, You put everything on earth that I would need, both to sustain my life and to atone for my sins. Thank You for loving me so very much! Help me, throughout my whole life, to grow in my love for You. Amen.

Genesis: In the Beginning— The First Seven Days

Lesson 8—The Sixth Day, Part II

Opening Prayer

Dear Creator God, thank You for giving us the book of Genesis and its beautiful description of Your amazing creation. Help me to realize that each of us has been lovingly, specially, and specifically created by You, and enable me to reflect You to the hurting world. In Jesus's name I pray. Amen.

1. Reread Genesis 1:27. The Concordia Self-Study Bible comments on this verse:

This highly significant verse is the first occurrence of poetry in the Old Testament (which is about 40% poetry). The word *created* is used three times in this verse to describe this central, divine act of the sixth day. *Male* and *female* alike bear the image of God and together they share in God's divine benediction— flourishing, filling the earth with its kind and exercising dominion over all the other earthly creatures. Man was created to be the steward of God's creatures.

The verse that was just read, Genesis 1:27, states that God *created* people in His own image. Now read Genesis 2:7, which gives a more detailed description of how this aspect of creation took place. Before God created human beings, each thing that God had created—light, evening and morning, the expanse of sky, oceans and dry ground, vegetation, sun, moon and stars, fish, birds and animals—had been made by

God's declaration, "Let there be ...." But human beings were specially formed by God from the dust of the ground, made in His image, and given God's own breath of life.

2. Does the creation story, especially the creation of people, have anything to do with our lives in this second millennium? Yes, according to Isaiah 55:6–13. The world that God created gives us a picture of His promise of salvation. Read those verses.

3. The book of Isaiah has further comments about creation. God reminds us that He is the only God, the eternal God, and that it is through Him that we have a Savior. Read His words in Isaiah 43:10–11.

4. God created people to praise Him, and He promises to provide for their needs in Isaiah 43:20–21.

5. Other verses found in Isaiah also speak of salvation in creation terms. Read Isaiah 45:8 and 61:11.

6. Created earth will not last forever, but God's promise of salvation is an eternal promise. Read Isaiah 51:6.

The promise that God's Word will last forever is repeated in the New Testament. Read Jesus's words in Matthew 24:35 and God's words about His Son in Hebrews 1:10–12. Also read Psalm 102:25–28 and finally Hebrews 13:8.

Closing Prayer

Dear LORD,

Thank you for creating me, loving me in spite of my sins, saving me, and promising to care for me for eternity. Through Your Holy Spirit, help me to cling to Your promise that no matter what change and decay I may observe developing throughout the world, You will never change. In the name of Your Son, my Savior Jesus,

I pray. Amen.

Genesis: In the Beginning—
The First Seven Days

Lesson 9—The Seventh Day

Opening Prayer

Dear Father God,

Thank You for Your Word, which teaches me how I can grow in a personal relationship with You. Through Your Holy Spirit, help me to grow both in my faith and in my joy of worship. I pray in the name of Your Son, Jesus. Amen.

1. Read Genesis 2:1–3. The Concordia Self-study Bible has this comment: "God rested on the seventh day, not because He was weary, but because nothing formless or empty remained. His creative work was completed—and it was totally effective, absolutely perfect, 'very good.' It did not have to be repeated, repaired or revised, and the Creator rested to commemorate it."

The first week of the world's existence occurred thousands of years ago. Then, it was perfect. We who are now living in the second millennium are very aware of the evils in the world. How can we relate to a perfect God and to something that happened so long ago? Read Isaiah 55:6–13.

2. Genesis 2:3 states that God blessed the seventh day and then, by resting from His work, made the day holy. The Hebrew word used for "rest" is the same word used for "Sabbath," found first in Exodus 16:23. Read that verse.

3. God used the Sabbath day, the day of rest, as a sign of the promise, known as a covenant, that He made with all people. Read also Exodus 20:11 and Genesis 9:12.

4. There have been some interesting observations made about the number seven throughout the scriptures:

In the original Hebrew language, Genesis 1:1 is comprised of seven words.
God declared, as recorded in Genesis 2:3, that the seventh day is holy.
The earth that God created has seven continents and seven oceans.
There are seven stars in the Big Dipper constellation.
There are seven colors in the rainbow.
There are seven notes in a musical scale.

More than five hundred times in the Bible, the number seven represents the completeness. Some examples follow:

God told Joshua and the people to march around Jericho seven times (see Joshua 6:4).
God reserved seven thousand faithful people in Israel (see 1 Kings 19:18 and Romans 11:4).
Seven sins that are detestable to God are listed in Proverbs 6:16–19.
Jesus talks about seven evil spirits in Luke 11:26
The book of Revelation, revealed to John, was directed to seven churches in Asia (see Revelation 1:4).

5. After reading both the Genesis account of creation and other scripture references to the very first week, we may wonder *why* God created us and just *what* our purpose is. The Bible gives many examples of God's communication with humankind, with the purpose of His created people

developing an eternal relationship with Him. The writing of the entire Bible was inspired by the Holy Ghost, the third person of the Trinity (read 2 Peter 1:21). To those who seek to know God, the Holy Spirit reveals through God's Word what they need to know. Read 1 Corinthians 1:18 and 1 Corinthians 2:9–13.

6. Even if we do not read and/or understand the entire Bible, our eternal relationship with God the Creator depends upon accepting His Son, Jesus, as the Savior who redeems us from our sins. When we repent of our sins and accept the sacrifice of His Son in our place, we are restored, in the eyes of God the Father, to the perfection that the very first created people enjoyed before sin entered the world. Our blessing is that through Jesus, we, who are sinful people, are able to again have a personal relationship with our perfect God. Read John 3:16 and 36 and John 5:19–24.

Closing Prayer

Dear Heavenly Father,

Thank You for creating me, for loving me so much, and for sacrificing Your Son, Jesus, as the way to restore me to the perfection of Your beautiful creation. Through Your Holy Spirit, keep my faith strong. Help me to do what I can to both enjoy and care for Your beautiful world. Don't allow Satan and the cares of the world to cause me to ever doubt Your love for me. Fill me with joy and keep my focus on the promise of spending eternity in perfection with You. Thank You again for Your amazing and personal love for me! Amen.

Introducing Old and New Testament Verses and Devotions

The original Bible, both Old and New Testaments, was written in Hebrew and Greek. Original attempts of translation were often marred by mistakes, caused by fourteen centuries of handwritten manuscripts of copying.

Eventually, both the Old and New Testaments were translated into many—but still not all—languages. In the English language, there are several popular translations; the King James Version (KJV), the Revised Standard Version (RSV), the New International Version (NIV), the New American Standard Version (NASV), and The Living Bible (TLB) translations are the most popular. In this book, the translations that are used are shown, but you are welcome to read from whatever translation you are using.

The Old Testament includes thirty-nine books. The final one, Malachi, was written four hundred years before God's Son, Jesus, came down to earth. The New Testament, with twenty-seven books, tells the story of Jesus and His earthly ministry of salvation. It then continues with the stories of the early years of Christian growth on earth, and it ends with the revelation of eternity with our Lord.

Everything that is written in God's Word is worth reading, studying, and applying to our lives. The following section of this book puts a focus on eleven passages from the Old Testament and twenty-seven passages from the New Testament, each followed by a devotion. As you read these, may God bless you and help you apply His Word to your life.

Our Heavenly Father's Redeeming Love

Then the man and his wife heard the sound of the
Lord God as he was walking in the garden in the cool
of the day, and they hid from the Lord God among the
trees of the garden. ... The Lord God made garments
of skin for Adam and his wife and clothed them.
—Genesis 3:8, 21 (NIV)

One day when I was ten years old, Mother needed to go to the grocery store. She asked me to finish washing the dishes while she was gone.

As I stood with my hands in the soapy water, I glanced up to the cabinet above the sink and realized that the bag of chocolate chips was kept there. I knew that I was not to eat them. But Mother was gone, so who would know?

I dried my hands, opened the bag, and poured out a handful of chocolate. Yum! Just then, the back door opened, and Mother walked in, catching me in my sinful act. I can still feel my cheeks getting hot with shame. Of course, I was punished, but I was also forgiven, and my mother still loved me. What a blessing!

I can't begin to imagine the fear and shame that Adam and Eve endured when they were caught in sin by their heavenly Father—the first sin to occur in God's beautiful, perfect world, the beginning of so much ruin and devastation. Yes, they were punished! We can read all about that in Genesis 2:14–24.

Yet, in spite of their sin, God continued to love Adam and Eve, and He gave them a promise of salvation (Genesis 2:15). Then, in His love for them, God Himself sacrificed animals of His perfect creation to make clothing for them from the animal skins. This beautiful gift of love was a tiny glimpse of the amazing sacrifice that God would do for each one of us through the death and blood of His perfect Son, Jesus.

We, like Adam and Eve, have been forgiven, and we can look forward to spending eternity with God and all of our Christian family in the perfection of heaven. Let this be our focus as we study God's Word.

Thank You, God, for Your forgiveness and Your eternal love for me! Amen.

A Sad Story with a Happy Ending

The Lord saw how great man's wickedness on the
earth had become, and that every inclination of the
thoughts of his heart was only evil all the time.
—Genesis 6:5 (NIV)

Which of these scenarios actually happened?

1. Anna May took her poinsettia home from church when the service ended. Within a week, its leaves began to drop off. *Oh, well. Christmas is over anyway*, she thought as she tossed the plant into the garbage can.

2. "I saw a cockroach in the kitchen!" shrieked the housewife. "Don't worry, ma'am," assured the exterminator. "We'll eliminate all of 'em."

3. "First he grew his hair long, then he dabbled in drugs, and now he says he's marrying a Jewish girl!" stormed the dad. "OK, dear, tomorrow we'll contact the lawyer and write our son out of the will."

4. "Grandma has Alzheimer's and doesn't know any of us. And now she has pneumonia? Just let her die."

5. "We already have four children and are barely squeaking by. And now I'm pregnant again? We'll have to abort this one!"

6. The Triune God made man in His own image, but in a very short time, He saw how great the wickedness on earth had become. The Lord was grieved that He had created people,

so He declared, "I will wipe mankind, whom I have created, from the face of the earth!" (Read Genesis 6:6 and 7.)

Oh, dear Lord, each one of the above stories is true! And I confess with great sorrow, as did Isaiah in chapter 6:5 of his book, that I am a part of the problem. I thank and praise You that You spared the human race through Noah and the flood of waters and that You have spared me through the waters of baptism. I am not expendable. You have redeemed me! What joy fills my heart as I think about it! Help me to always keep my confidence in You as I learn more about You through Your holy Word. Amen.

God's Wonderful Promises

The Lord stood beside (Jacob) and said, "I AM the Lord,
the God of Abraham and of our father Isaac. The ground
you are lying on is yours! I will give it to you and to
your descendants ... I will be with you constantly until
I have finished giving you all that I am promising."
—Genesis 28:13 and 15 (TLB)

When I was pregnant with my second child, digital clocks became popular. Several months into my pregnancy, I began to see my clock at 11:11 every morning and every night. I began to think that these numbers must be showing me a Bible verse that would be meaningful to my expected baby.

It took quite a bit of searching through all of the Bible's books before I found the very meaningful passage. In 1 Samuel 1:11, Hannah prayed, "O Lord of heaven, if You will look down upon my sorrow and answer my prayer and give me a son, then I will give him back to You, and he'll be yours for his entire lifetime" (TLB). I instantly interpreted this as a promise from God that my son-to-be would serve Him with his life.

Andrew was a very intelligent boy and a very talented musician, and I often wondered where this would lead him. Would he become a pastor or a missionary? No! He became a restaurant worker!

But Andrew also became an active musician in his church. His wife, Sara, became a worker for Youth for Christ, an outreach founded by Billy Graham, to unmarried teenaged parents. Beside their own three children, Andrew and Sara have cared for many foster children. For several months, they housed a sixteen–year-old boy and his newborn baby daughter! They are now in the process of officially adopting two foster children whom they have housed for several years since their births.

Has this been easy? Definitely not! But they continually feel from God the same promise that He gave to Jacob, "I will be with you constantly." The Christian faith that they have shared with their own three children, the many teenaged parents, and the many foster children has been an amazing reflection of God's love!

And God offers this same wonderful promise to each of us. The more we study His Word and talk to Him in prayer, the more our close relationship grows with Him. And that is a *promise*!

Dear Lord, thank You so much for the love, forgiveness, salvation, and guidance that You share with me each day. Keep me close to You through Your Word. In Jesus's name. Amen.

Music Is a Glorious Gift from God!

Read Exodus 15:1–18. (If time is short, read verse 2.)

> The Lord is my strength and my song. He is my Savior.
> This is my God and I will praise Him, my father's God and
> I will honor Him. (NKJV)

Exodus chapter 15:1–18 records the words of a beautiful song that Moses and the Israelites sang to the Lord after God rescued them from the terror and persecution of Pharaoh and the Egyptians. All the glory is given to the Lord.

Interestingly, 1 Corinthians 10:1–4 tells us to learn from what happened during this rescue. It says that the Israelites were all united with Moses by baptism in the cloud and in the sea and that the spiritual rock from which they drank was Christ.

Hebrews 11 tells us, in verses 24–26, that Moses, who was raised with faith in the one true God, gave up his position as a son of Pharaoh's daughter because he thought that being insulted for Christ would be better than having the treasurers of Egypt, and he looked forward to his reward. As we can see from these verses (and many others in the Old Testament), everything that happened was pointing to salvation by Christ. And even though the Israelites didn't know what God's future plan was, they were inspired to praise God with music and song. We should look at God that same way!

Exodus 15:2 states that God is "my father's God." Since my earthly father died, my relationship with my heavenly Dad has grown even closer! I thank Him for the gift of music every single day! Music, first mentioned in Genesis 4:21, is a beautiful, calming, encouraging, inspiring, glorious gift from God. Whether we sing, play instruments, or simply listen to it, music is a marvelous way that we can connect with our heavenly Father and His eternal, personal love for us.

The song recorded in Exodus 15 includes these wonderful words: "Lovingly, You will lead the people You have saved (redeemed). Powerfully, You will guide them to Your holy dwelling." What a wonderful promise this is to each of us, His children!

O Lord, thank You for being my heavenly Dad, for loving me as Your child, and for filling my life with music! You are my strength and song, and You have redeemed me. Thank You! In Jesus's name I pray. Amen.

Knowing God Personally

> Whenever Moses went into the Tabernacle ... a pillar of
> cloud would come down and stand at the door while the
> Lord spoke with Moses. Inside the tent the Lord spoke
> to Moses face to face, as a man speaks to his friend.
> —Exodus 33:8–9, 11 (TLB)

What awe did Moses feel while he spoke face-to-face with the Lord? Exodus 34 tells us that when Moses came down the mountain after spending forty days and forty nights with God, his face glowed from having been in God's presence.

The Bible tells of others who had close, personal relationships with the Lord: Adam and Eve in Genesis 1–2; Abraham in Genesis 17–18. The four Gospels tell us of many people who interacted with Jesus, God's Son who came to earth in human form. Acts 9 and 22 tell of Paul's personal meeting with Jesus on earth, after Jesus had previously died, risen, and returned to heaven! In Acts 8:34–36, we read that Stephen, while being stoned and executed for his faith, was welcomed personally into heaven by Jesus.

Throughout the New Testament, Christians are continually reminded to be lights to the world, reflections of God's love, mercy, and forgiveness. Ephesians 4:1–3 and 32 and Colossians 3:18–21 are examples of this command. Is this always easy? No! But Philippians 1:12–14 and 4:8 show us a beautiful example of reflecting Christ's love: Peter was so filled with faith and joy, even while in prison and in chains, that other prisoners also became Christians!

Our heavenly Father loves *each one of us* personally and desires our relationship, just as He did with Moses and Peter. The more we read God's Word, the closer this relationship grows.

Do you know a Christian whose life is a witness of God's love and grace? When my friend's eighth-grade daughter died of asthma, she used this death to witness of Anna's faith and salvation to all of the hospital workers. When my father spent the final year of WWII in the Stalag Luft III prison camp, he continually encouraged the other prisoners through his faith. While one of my church's pastors experienced painful issues with his hips, he continued to serve our church with his faith, sermons, and leadership.

Is your life a daily reflection of knowing Jesus? Read God's Word and talk to Him every day. You, too, will experience a close, loving, personal relationship with the Lord!

Dear God, please help me to continually grow even closer to You through Your Word, and help me to be a light and reflection of You to the world around me. In Jesus's name. Amen.

Almighty God, Please Give Me the Strength!

> Read Judges chapter 16:23–31. Then focus on verse 28: "Then Samson prayed to the Lord, 'O Sovereign Lord, remember me. O God, please strengthen me just once more, and let me with one blow get revenge on the Philistines for my two eyes'" (NIV).

Do you know the story of Samson?

His story, written in Judges chapters 13 through 17, is interesting, amazing, and filled with examples of God's love and care for sinful people whom He created. I greatly encourage you to read these five chapters!

First, a messenger of the Lord appeared to a barren wife and promised that she would become pregnant with a son! God's messenger also told her exactly how to raise him. When the baby was born, his mother named him Samson, and the Lord blessed him.

As Samson grew up, he was incredibly muscular and strong. He was also sinful. Eventually he experienced punishment from God. He was captured by the Philistines, who poked out his eyes, took him to prison, tied him up with double chains, and forced him to work as a grain grinder.

While he experienced this punishment, Samson also began to grow again in faith. He called out to God, "Almighty Lord, please remember me! God, give me strength just one more time!" And God responded by perhaps giving Samson more strength than anyone else on earth has ever had! The strength caused the death of thousands of God-rejecting Philistines. Samson died too—and entered eternity with the Lord.

We are sinners too. So we can be encouraged by Samson's unique story. God planned each of our lives. He loves us, and He is always ready to help us and to forgive our sins when we turn to Him!

Dear Lord, thank You for creating me and loving me. And thank You for forgiving my sins! Help me to grow in my faith every day. In Jesus's name. Amen.

We Must Confess Our Sins

Read 2 Samuel 12:1–13. Then focus on verse 13: "Then David said to Nathan, 'I have sinned against the Lord'" (NIV).

You have undoubtedly read or heard the story of David. He was raised as a shepherd, he killed Goliath the giant, he became rich, and he became the wonderful king of Israel. The Bible tells us, in 2 Samuel 8:14, that "everywhere David went, the Lord gave him victories."

But as David grew more powerful as the king, he began to put his focus on his own desires and accomplishments, rather than seeking God's guidance and wisdom. God responded with anger and punishment, asking David, through the prophet Nathan, "Why did you despise My Word by doing what I considered evil?" (read 2 Samuel 9).

David responded with guilt and shame, "I have sinned against the Lord" (v. 13).

Have you ever become so involved with an area of your life that you have left God out of your focus and decisions? It is very easy to do! When we fail to pray and ask God for His guidance every day, we, too, as did David, fall into sin.

Thankfully, when we realize our sins and confess them to God, He does forgive us. Nathan told David, "The Lord has taken away your sin" (v. 13). What a blessing for David—and for each of us! This is why Jesus died on the cross. He paid for our sins! We may still endure punishment, just as David did. But when we confess our sins, our relationship with our heavenly Father is fully restored!

Dear Lord, I do confess that I am sinful. Help me to keep my daily focus more on You and Your guidance. Thank You for loving me, and thank You so much for forgiving me! In Jesus's name I pray. Amen.

Naaman Healed of Leprosy / A Little Child Shall Lead Them

Read 2 Kings chapter 5 and then focus on verse 3: "One day the little girl said to her mistress, 'I wish my master would go to see the prophet in Samaria. He would heal him of his leprosy'" (TLB).

Chapter 5 is chock-full of people who faced challenges!

The Israelites were challenged by invading bands of Syrians.

Naaman was humbled and challenged by an invasion of leprosy into his life.

The king was insulted and challenged by the impossible request that he heal Naaman!

Elisha was challenged to respond to the king and witness to the awesome power of God.

Naaman's officers were challenged to boldly reason with Naaman, their commander in chief, when he was so distraught.

Gehazi, Elisha's servant, was tempted and challenged by the opportunity to get rich quickly.

But I find myself challenged by the simple statement of the little captive girl who, in verse 3, said to Naaman's wife, "I wish my master would go to see the prophet in Samaria. He would heal him of his leprosy!" Her simple wish led her master to the Lord, where Naaman experienced healing of body, mind, and spirit as he came to faith in the one true God.

Our challenge is to share this story with the children that we know. How wonderful and affirming it is to our young people that God does not have to wait for us to be all grown-up to be workers in His harvest field. In fact, I challenge you to seek out other Bible stories in which God uses children; then read them to your own boys and girls. Show them from the scriptures that they are already an important part of God's kingdom work!

Dear Lord and Author of my faith, thank You for showing me through Your holy Word that I am a valued child of Yours, no matter what my age! In Jesus's name. Amen.

From Fear to Honor

Read Esther 5:9–14 and 6:1–11. Then put your focus on Esther 6:11, "This is what is done for the man the king delights to honor!" (NIV).

The story of Mordecai in this book reminds me of my father's story during WWII. He became a B17 pilot, even after enduring a horrific airplane crash during his training, an event that killed his instructor and left my father with a crushed pelvis, lost teeth, and some unconscious days. Even so, he recovered enough to earn his pilot's license, and he then accomplished many successful war experiences. Eventually, though, his plane was shot down. He successfully landed in Packebusch, a German potato field. No one was killed, but all were taken to prison camps. My father spent the final year of WWII at Stalag Luft III, enduring one of the coldest winters on record, including a thirty-hour march to a different camp, Mooseburg, where he was eventually liberated at the war's end.

Forty years later, the mayor of Packebusch invited my father to come to that town to give a presentation and to be honored as "the one who brought fame to Packebusch"! Over the next thirty years, my dad continued to be honored in many ways for his amazing accomplishments. He always gave God the glory and used his life as a Christian outreach in many ways.

The Bible is filled with lessons that apply to our own lives. It teaches that God, our heavenly Father, has honored each of us through His Son, Jesus, whose death paid the penalty for all of our sins. We do not have to fear eternal punishment for our sins, because, through Jesus's death, God no longer even remembers our sins (see Hebrews 8:12)!

The blessings of attending church services is that as we read God's Word, sing hymns based on Bible verses, and spend time with other believers, our faith is encouraged, and we become equipped to live as witnesses of Jesus's love and salvation, even when things don't seem to be going well. God promises in His Word that He will *never* leave us or forsake us (Deuteronomy 31:6)!

Dear Lord, thank You for all the stories in the Bible that teach us of Your wonderful, redeeming love. Help me to be a witness of Your love and salvation to other people around me. In the name of Your wonderful Son, Jesus, I pray. Amen.

"All Things Have Become New!"

"This is the covenant I will make with the house of
Israel after that time", declared the Lord. "I will put
my law in their minds and write it on their hearts. I
will be their God and they will be My people."
—Jeremiah 31:33 (NIV)

The indescribable beauty of the Old Testament tabernacle
and its exquisite furnishings awed the children of Israel. God
Himself had designed every detail. Why, He had even endowed
two craftsmen with His special Spirit and extraordinary artistic
skills to oversee the production of this incredibly beautiful tent
of worship. Then God appointed high priests to represent the
people before their holy God to atone for the sins of the people.
Finally, God had written His commandments on stone tablets
with His own finger, so that the Israelites would know exactly
what was required of them.

But in spite of many ceremonies and sacrifices, the children of
Israel repeatedly fell away from God. Their priests were sinners
too. They simply couldn't keep their part of the covenant. (You
can read all about this in Exodus chapters 25–31.)

So, when the time was right, God sent Jesus, His own Son, to
the sinful world. Jesus kept all of the commandments perfectly.
He appealed to the Holy God as the perfect high priest. He gave
Himself as the perfect sacrifice. As a result, God declared a new
covenant, one that replaced the one from Moses's time. The new
promise had superior benefits. Now God's people could delight
in having fellowship with God and doing His will. Forgiveness of
sins would be an everlasting reality. (Read Hebrews chapter 8.)

You and I are so blessed to be people of the new promise! We are free to worship God in a relationship of love, not an attitude of fear. Because Jesus paid it all, nothing is required of us. But the more we experience the indescribable love and acceptance of God, the more we want to give everything back to Him! I encourage you to read Jeremiah 31:33–37 and praise God for including *you* as one of his chosen people!

Dear Lord Almighty, Creator of all, with joy I thank You for loving me, forgiving me, and claiming me as Your child! Help me to always look at You as my heavenly Dad! In Jesus's name. Amen.

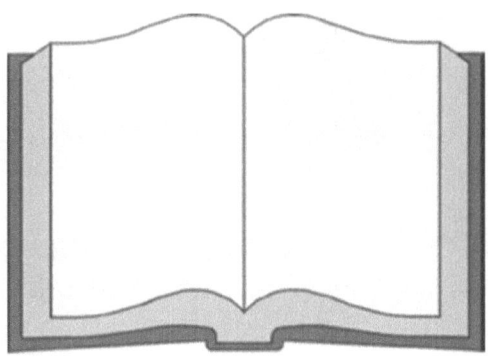

The Blessing of Self-Control

Be self-controlled and alert. Your enemy the devil prowls around like a roaring lion looking for someone to devour.
—1 Peter 5:8 (NIV)

1. When people disagree with me, (4) Lord, for my sinful state I grieve.

I can't get them my point to see, yet I despair not but believe.
And everyone will not agree. And full salvation I receive!
Lord, I pray—Lord, I pray—
Please give me self-control. Please give me self-control.

2. So many of the worldly cares (5). The *fruits* You mention in Galatians

Entrap me in their wily snares. I grasp with great anticipation
I need the discipline of prayers! And offer thanks with jubilation!
Lord, I pray—Lord, I pray—
Please give me self-control. Please give me self-control.

3. If spiritual armor I should lack (6), as I progress from year to year

And thus expose my front or back and see my end of days draw near,
So Satan's able to attack, or wait for Christ to reappear,
Lord, I pray—Lord, I pray—
Please give me self-control. Please give me self-control. Amen.

These are the Bible references for each verse:
#1—Titus 1:8 and 2:2, 5, 6, 12
#2—1 Peter 4:7

#3—1 Thessalonians 5:6, 8 and 1 Corinthians 7:5
#4—Acts 24:25
#5—Galatians 5:22

#6—Titus 2:12

The Guiding Star

After Jesus was born in Bethlehem in Judea, during the time
of King Herod, Magi from the east came to Jerusalem and
asked, "Where is the one who has been born king of the Jews?
We saw his star in the east and have come to worship him."
—Matthew 2:1–2 (NIV)

Much twenty-first-century technology is beyond some people's
grasp, but I am glad to live in an age where science explains and
supports many of the mysteries revealed in God's Word. The
story of Gentile men being invited to meet Jesus, God's Son, their
King, is a thrilling story to me for two reasons: First, I am also
a Gentile, and second, five of my favorite words in the Bible are
"He made the stars, also" (Genesis 1:16).

For many centuries, people have speculated about the "star
of wonder." In our age of the Hubble telescope, much has been
revealed about the universe, including the stars and planets in
our own solar system. Astronomers can now look back in history
to see exactly what was happening in the sky on any given date.
Here is what they have discovered:

God used the planets to guide the magi, the wise men, to Jesus.
Jupiter, the "planet of kings," was in such a close conjunction with
Venus, the "mother planet," that it appeared to men's eyes as the
most brilliant star that had ever been seen! It traveled ahead of
the magi as they went south from Jerusalem to Bethlehem. Then,
amazingly, as it entered its retrograde, Jupiter appeared to stop
in the sky over the town of Bethlehem.

What God the Creator put into the sky when "He created the
stars, also" is a picture of unimaginable, awesome beauty! And

it includes both the times of Jesus's birth and crucifixion! In Acts 2:14–21, Peter quotes a prophecy of Joel that includes a prediction of blood, fire, smoke, and a blood moon that would happen in the sky at the time of the Savior's death. All of this was fulfilled when Jesus shed His blood on the cross: when lightning (fire) and storm clouds (smoke) and darkness filled the sky and when a lunar eclipse on that date caused the moon to appear as blood red. This has been proven to have occurred on April 3, AD 33.

Even before God created people, He put His plan of salvation into the universe as proof of His amazing love for each of us! Gentiles as well as Jews are invited to meet Jesus, accept Him as their Savior, and live as His disciples.

Dear Lord, please don't ever let me doubt Your eternal and personal love for me! Thank You that I can learn about Your love through Your Word. In Jesus's name. Amen.

Herod's Terrible Plan

Read Matthew 2:3–8 and verses 16–18. Verse 16 tells us that "Herod was furious when he learned that the astrologers had disobeyed him. Sending soldiers to Bethlehem, he ordered them to kill every baby boy two years old and under, both in the town and on the nearby farms, for the astrologers had told him that the star first appeared two years before" (TLB).

"I am the king!" Herod reminded himself. "The power and authority belong to me! No one will take this away from me!" But the words rang hollow and empty within his own heart. The wise men from the east had spoken of a *new* king whose sign was in the heavens, signaled by a special star. Then the chief priests and scribes confirmed that this had indeed been foretold by the prophets. Herod slammed his fist into his palm. How could he fight against the stars?

Fear gnawed at Herod's heart as he paced and thought. Suddenly, he had a plan. A plan! Of course! Hadn't the wise men said that this new king was yet a baby? Born in Bethlehem, they had said. And then they'd had the audacity not to return to the palace! But Herod couldn't be bothered with those thoughts just now. He had to develop the plan. Oh! How easy! How complete! He'd have his soldiers kill all the Bethlehem babies, all the baby boys up to one year old. Herod rubbed his hands in satisfaction. But his palms grew cold and clammy. That fear! It kept rising in his stomach. So Herod expanded his plan: the soldiers could kill all the male babies up to *two* years old. *Curse the star!* thought Herod. *I am the king!*

God had a plan, too, a plan that was filled with love much, much stronger than all of Herod's fear. An army of murdering soldiers could not stop God's plan for bringing salvation to His people. The new baby King was Jesus, God's only Son, a gift of love for the whole world, to Herod, to you, to me. Herod refused to acknowledge Jesus, and so he never knew peace. What is *your* response to Jesus?

Dear Lord God, thank You for Your perfect plan. Please grant to me that peace that the world cannot give. Set my heart to obey Your commandments with joy and thanksgiving for the wonderful gift of salvation You have given to me through Jesus. In His name I pray. Amen.

Looking Ahead to the Kingdom of Heaven

From that time on Jesus began to preach, "Repent,
for the Kingdom of Heaven has come near."
—Matthew 4:17 (NIV)

Jesus did not say that all we need to do to inherit eternal life is to believe in Him. He also told us that we need to repent. What does that really mean for us?

The dictionary explains that to repent means to "turn from sin." But this is not something we can do by ourselves, because every one of us is sinful! It is only when we put our true faith in Jesus, who gave His life to free us from our sins, that we can learn to repent.

God gave us ten commandments, as recorded in Exodus 20:3–17, that He demands for us to obey. Jesus tells us that if one of us breaks even the least of one of these commandments, that person will be the least in the kingdom of heaven! (See Matthew 5:17–19.)

Have you ever decided to stay home from church on a Sunday? Did you ever disobey your parents? Have you ever taken something that belongs to someone else? Or told a lie? Or been envious of what others own but you do not? These, and many other actions of ours, are sins! We need to repent—to admit our sins to Jesus and to those whom we have sinned against—and ask Jesus to help us to not commit those sins again.

Dear Jesus, I thank You with all my heart that You love me and died to save me from my sins. Help me to turn from my sins and to grow daily closer to You through Your Word. I really do look forward to living with You in heaven some day! Amen.

The Power of Peace

Blessed are the peacemakers, for they
will be called sons of God.
—Matthew 5:9 (NIV)

Satan is overjoyed when our hearts are faint with fear. Daily headlines remind us that people are destroying themselves with hatred and violence. Terrorism keeps hitting closer to home, and nations threaten war. Family conflicts erode our home lives, and diseases attack our bodies. Satan laughs when humankind is filled with insecurity, doubt, and dread.

No one felt that despair more than the disciples, who hid together in fear in a locked room after Jesus's crucifixion. Their Messiah was dead, their hopes dashed, and they feared for their lives. Then suddenly, miraculously, the living LORD appeared in their midst, greeting them with these words: "Peace be with you!" This changed everything!

Jesus comes into our world with the same blessing: "Peace be with you!" As Satan flees in defeat, our hearts are flooded with Jesus's perfect love, which casts out fear (1 John 4:18). Renewed by God's perfect peace, we can now live joyful lives in spite of sickness and disease

(1 Thessalonians 5:16–18). We can live in forgiveness and fellowship with family members (Colossians 3:13–14). We can pray with confidence, knowing that God is in control of the affairs of nations (Psalm 47:1). And we can eagerly tell of the hope that is in us to anyone who asks about our source of peace (Colossians 4:2–6).

We need only to open the eyes of our hearts to see that Jesus, our Savior, is in the room with us, as He was with the disciples. We can hear Him say to us, "Peace be with you!" (see also John 14:27). By experiencing the peace of Christ, we have truly been blessed to be a blessing to others!

Lord Jesus, with Your peace in my heart, I am freed from Satan's lies that would bind me to fear. Empower me to be a bold witness of Your peace, in the hope that through me, God will grant repentance to others, "leading them to a knowledge of the truth, and that they will come to their senses and escape from the trap of the devil, who has taken them captive to do his will." (See 2 Timothy 4:25–26.)

Lord, I Want to Be a Tree

Here is another of Jesus's illustrations: "The kingdom of Heaven is like a tiny mustard seed planted in the field. It is the smallest of all the seeds, but becomes the largest of plants, and grows into a tree where birds can come and find shelter" (Matthew 13:11–12 TLB).

I have loved hearing and reading God's holy Word ever since I was a very little girl, when my mother read the entire Bible to me. My favorite story has always been the account of the creation of the world. Throughout my life. I have continued to study and be awed and amazed by God's incredible science and artistry. His creative accomplishments will never be fully understood by humans. He is vastly bigger than we are, yet God's love for each of us is intensely personal. The more I study His Word, the more I am humbled by His amazing love for me.

Throughout my childhood, I memorized many Bible verses, a goodly number from the book of Psalms. One of my very favorites is Psalm 1:1–3, "Blessed is the person who does not follow the advice of wicked people, take the path of sinners, or join the company of mockers. Rather, he delights in the teachings of the Lord and reflects on His teachings day and night. *He is like a tree planted beside streams—a tree that produces fruit in season and whose leaves do not wither.* He succeeds in everything he does" (RSV).

I am a product of God's marvelous creation, and I have always received comfort and encouragement from those verses. And I find it interesting that God's Son, my Savior, Jesus, is referred to in this same picture as prophesied in Isaiah 11:1: "There shall come forth a shoot from the stump of Jesse, and a branch shall grow out of his roots" (RSV).

God has used me through many phases of my life to produce fruit for Him, to be a witness of His love and salvation, and to be an encouragement to others who are seeking God's love and guidance. But I have also gone through seasons of stress and depression, when I wonder if I am accomplishing anything of value for the Lord. During those dry times, I cling to the words of Jeremiah 17:7–8: "Blessed is the man who trusts in the Lord, whose trust is the Lord. "He is like a tree that is planted by water, that sends out its roots by the stream, and does not fear when heat comes, for its leaves remain green. It will not be anxious during droughts, for it does not cease to bear fruit" (RSV).

I have always been awed, humbled, and amazed that the holy, mighty Maker of the world included me in His creation, that He has nurtured me and encouraged me through His Word ever since I was a tiny seed, and that He has an eternal plan for me as I continue to grow in His perfect love and guidance. This I believe!

Dear Lord, thank You for planting *me* as a tiny seed in Your marvelous creation! Help me to grow and be a witness of You throughout my whole earthly life. In Jesus's name. Amen.

Meeting God on the Mountaintop

Read the story in Matthew chapter 17. Then focus on verses 1–5.

> After six days Jesus took Peter, James and John (the brother of James) and led them up a high mountain by themselves. (NIV, verse 1)

When I was a girl in grade school, I could not relate at all to this story of Jesus on the mountaintop. *Transfiguration*—what a big word! Using the verses of a hymn by Joseph Robinson, who lived from 1838 to 1933, "How good, Lord, to be here," my father helped me to personalize the meaning of this story.

> How good, Lord, to be here! Your glory fills the night; Your face and garments, like the sun, shine with unborrowed light. How good, Lord, to be here! Your beauty to behold where Moses and Elijah stand, Your messengers of old. (Verses 1 and 2)

Peter, James, and John could scarcely believe their eyes at the glimpse of heaven they beheld: there stood Jesus, Son of man, in His perfect glory as the Son of God! The three disciples recognized Moses and Elijah—both alive and doing very well!—as though they had known these two long-dead men all their lives.

> Fulfiller of the past and hopes of things to be! We hail Your body glorified and our redemption see. (Verse 3)

As the disciples' sinful eyes began to absorb what they were witnessing, reality hit: this truly *is* the Savior, the Messiah, the one prophesied, our Redeemer from sin! Peter spoke for the three; they had tasted perfection from sin and wished to remain in that blessed state forever!

> Before we tase of death, we see Your kingdom come. We long to hold the vision bright and make this hill our home. (Verse 4)

Sometimes we, like the disciples, experience a very personal, meaningful time with the Lord and wish, oh so desperately, that we could hold that closeness forever. When we hear horror stories of crime, when our bodies suffer intense injury or illness, when we lose a loved one to death, we want nothing more than to abandon this sinful world for all the peace, joy, and promise of heaven!

> How good, Lord, to be here! Yet we may not remain; but since You bid us leave the mount, come with us to the plain. (Verse 5)

God has appointed a life span for each of us (Hebrews 9:27), and it's His decision if we should presently live on earth or in heaven. The joy is that Jesus does not *abandon* us to the sinful earth; He *returns* with us, as He did with Peter, James, and John. So, as Paul exclaimed, "For to me, to live is Christ and to die is gain" (Philippians 1:21 NIV).

Thank You, Lord Jesus, for walking with me during both my mountaintop and valley experiences. Thank You also for parents, teachers, and pastors who help me to better understand Your Word. Amen.

I Am Jesus's Little Lamb

If a man has 100 sheep, and one wanders away and is lost,
what will he do? Won't he leave the ninety-nine others and
go out into the hills to search for the lost one? And if he
finds it, he will rejoice over it more than over the ninety-
nine others safe at home! Just so, it is not my Father's
will that even one of these little ones should perish.
—Matthew 18:12–14 (TLB)

Did you learn the song, as shown in the title, when you were
little?

God created such a huge variety of animals! My Ohio grandparents
had many geese, ducks, chickens, cats, dogs, goats, pigs, cows, and
sheep. My siblings and I held and played with all of them, except
the sheep. They ran away from us every time we approached
them, and had they not been in a penned area, they would have
scattered and possibly never have been found.

Throughout the Old Testament, God ordered His people to
sacrifice healthy sheep to receive His forgiveness for their sins.
When Jesus came to earth as a human, He became the Lamb
of God who would be sacrificed for *our* sins. But our heavenly
Father also views each one of us as one of His precious sheep. If
one of us strays from our faith, He reaches out to us to bring us
back to His love and to restore our faith and salvation.

Is it really true that God loves each of us that much? Yes! He
created each of us individually, and not one of us is more or less
important to Him than anyone else. God wants every one of us
to be saved (1 Timothy 2:4–5).

70

So, "Ever glad at heart I am, for my Shepherd gently guides me, knows my needs and well provides me; loves me every day the same; even calls me by my name!"

Yes, that's true! (Read Isaiah 43:1.)

Dear Jesus, thank You so much for allowing Yourself to be sacrificed for me, and thank You for rescuing me and bringing me into Your family as one of Your precious lambs. I know that "when my short life is ended, by Your angel host attended, You will fold me to Your breast, safe within Your arms to rest." Amen.

(The text for this hymn, "I Am Jesus's Little Lamb" was written by Henrietta L. von Hayn, who lived from 1724 to 1782.)

Hosanna!

They brought the donkey and the colt, placed their cloaks
on them, and Jesus sat on them. A very large crowd spread
their cloaks on the road, while others cut branches from
the trees and spread them on the road. The crowds that
went ahead of Him and those that followed shouted,
"Hosanna to the Son of David!" "Blessed is He Who comes
in the name of the Lord!" "Hosanna in the highest!"
—Matthew 21:7–9 (NIV)

O Jesus, what was it really like for You that day as You rode into Jerusalem on that little donkey? Of course the Bible does not reveal all of Your thoughts, but I have often wondered if You were pondering some of the thoughts I have written here:

Did the words of the ancient prophecy, as recorded more than four hundred years earlier in Zechariah 9:9, keep going through Your head? "Rejoice greatly, O my people! Shout with joy! For look—your King is coming! He is the Righteous One, the Victor! Yet He is lowly, riding on a donkey's colt!" (TLB).

Were You filled with overwhelming love as You looked at Your disciples, who glowed with such excitement, hope, and pride?

Did You *feel* like a king or conqueror as Your way was strewn with coats and branches, signifying a royal highway?

Were You honored and exalted, perhaps even comforted, by the shouts of praise that greeted You as You passed by the crowds?

Did it anger You to witness the unbelief and hardened hearts of the chief priests and other Jewish leaders, or were You moved to feel pity and love?

O Jesus, could You hear Satan whispering to You as he had in the wilderness, "I will give You all this splendid honor and glory if You will only kneel and worship me" (Matthew 4:8–9 TLB)?

Jesus, could You feel the loving presence of Your Father, who said of You at Your baptism, "This is My beloved Son, in Whom I am well pleased!" (Matthew 3:17 RSV)?

O Jesus, what was it really like for You that day as You rode the little donkey into Jerusalem?

Did you ever think of *me*?

I thank You, Jesus, with all my heart, that You followed the straight and royal highway all the way to the cross, carrying all of my sins with You. Hosanna! Amen.

Follow the Father's Will

Read the story of Jesus's anguished prayer in the Garden of Gethsemane, as it is recorded in Matthew 26:36–46, which includes this plea: "My Father, if it is not possible for this cup to be taken away unless I drink it, may Your will be done" (NIV).

We all confess the Trinity, so we believe, as Jesus often stated, that He and the Father are one. For that reason, we sometimes find it hard to imagine the intense suffering that Jesus endured for our sakes. Didn't being God give Him an advantage?

As I pondered this, I decided to read all of Jesus's own statements that pertain to Him obeying His Father's will. I was amazed at how many references there are! When read all together, the love, devotion, honor, trust, and obedience that Jesus felt for His Father is overwhelming! I encourage you to use your Bible concordance and look up these references for yourself.

But as Jesus's time of sacrifice approached, though He never wavered in obedience and trust, He anguished as a man and pleaded with His Father to consider an alternate plan: "My Father, if it is not possible for this cup to be taken away unless I drink it, may Your will be done" (Matthew 26:42 NIV). And being in anguish, He prayed more earnestly, and His sweat was like drops of blood falling to the ground (Luke 22:44).

Jesus had the very faith He expressed in Mark 11:24: "Whatever you ask for in prayer, believe that you have received it and it will be yours" (NIV). Yet He trusted His Father's decision. "Father, I have brought You glory on earth by completing the work You gave Me to do" (John 17:4 NIV). "If I glorify Myself, My glory means nothing. My Father ... is the One Who glorifies Me" (John 8:54 NIV). "Now My heart is troubled, and what shall I say? Father, save Me from this hour? No, it was for this very reason that I came to this hour. Father, glorify Your Name!" (John 12:27–28 NIV).

We, too, love God and want to glorify His Name. To do so, our "attitude should be the same as that of Christ Jesus" (Philippians 2:5–11 NIV). We must be devoted to the Word and seek to know the will of God. Then, like Jesus, we will be given the power to love, honor, trust, and obey our Father.

Lord, Thank You for what Your Son, Jesus, did for me. Please help me to seek and accept Your will every day in my life. Amen.

Where Is Judas?

Read Matthew 27:1–10. Then focus on verse 5: "So Judas threw the money into the temple and left. Then he went away and hanged himself" (NIV).

In reading this story, I have always questioned Judas's salvation. Doing research about Judas has helped my understanding, and I hope it will help yours as well.

Matthew is the only Gospel writer who tells the story of Judas's death, so my research did include looking into other Gospels. In John 17:12, Jesus referred to Judas, saying that only one of His apostles became lost. In John 6:64–71, Jesus said that Judas, although acting as a disciple, had never been a believer.

The Nelson Study Bible states that Judas was wholly responsible for his own actions. He opened his own heart to Satan, as reported in John 13:27. The Reformation Study Bible says that Judas's refusal to respond to Jesus's appeal opened his heart to Satan's control and surrendered his heart to the dominion of evil. In John 12:6, Judas is referred to as a thief. And in 1 Corinthians 6:9–11, the apostle Paul lists thievery as one of the sins that shuts people out of the kingdom of God.

Judas, along with many other people, met Jesus and experienced the support of the church. All of the apostles were sinners. One of the most grievous sins occurred during Jesus's mock trial, when Peter, Jesus's close and trusted friend, denied three times, with oaths and swearing, that he even *knew* Jesus!

The sins of both Judas and Peter had been predicted by Jesus ahead of time. Peter repented of his sins and was totally forgiven by the Lord. Judas could also have repented, but he did not; he died in his sin, without asking for or receiving forgiveness.

Throughout the centuries, many people, including us, have met Jesus and have experienced the support of the church. But have we truly admitted and confessed our sins to Jesus? Do we live as Peter, truly asking God for—and receiving—His forgiveness and the promise of salvation? Or do we live—and die—as Judas?

Let us each examine our own hearts and live as forgiven, redeemed, and joyful disciples of our wonderful, personal Savior, Jesus!

Dear Jesus, I am truly sorry for all of the times that I sin! Thank You for dying on the cross to save me for eternity! Help me to live my life as a reflection to others of Your wonderful love and forgiveness. Amen.

The New Covenant

As they were eating, Jesus took bread and asked God's blessing on it and broke it in pieces and gave it to them and said, "Eat it—this is My body." Then He took a cup of wine and gave thanks to God for it and gave it to them, and they all drank from it. And He said to them, "This is my blood, poured out for many, sealing the new covenant between God and man. I solemnly declare that I shall never again taste wine until the day I drink a different kind in the Kingdom of God."
—Mark 14:22–25 (TLB)

What wondrous words our Savior spoke
As the Passover bread He broke:
"This is My body given for you,
Soon to be broken; then made new.
I'll *always* be with you, though raised on a tree.
So take it and eat, in remembrance of Me."

Then Jesus lifted the Passover cup.
After thanks to the Lord had been lifted up,
He invited each of them to drink of the wine.
"This is My blood," He said. "I am the vine.
I promise you that if you're grafted to Me,
We will each live together in eternity."

(Based on Mark 14:22–25.)

Dear Lord Jesus, thank You for Your wonderful gift of the Lord's Supper. Help me to cling to the promise that it offers of spending my eternal life with You in heaven! Amen.

Netting a Prize Catch

Read Luke 5:4–11.

> "Master, we have toiled all the night, and have taken nothing; nevertheless, at Your Word I will let down the net" (Verse 5 NKJV).

A church that we were members of had a children's fish pond at its annual summer picnic. What a spot of excitement it was! Scores of little children lined up in front of the tall, colorful blanket, waiting for a turn to throw the fishing line over the top. No one knew what the prize would be, but everyone was guaranteed a catch.

Early in Jesus's ministry, He told a group of fishermen to "launch out into the deep and let down your nets for a catch." The men were weary; they had fished all night and had caught nothing. Yet they heard the promise in Jesus's words. So they let down their net, and this time their nets were filled to the breaking point! In fact, the boat began to sink!

The fishermen were astonished and overwhelmed. Jesus calmed their fearful hearts and then gave them an amazing promise: "From now on, you will catch *men*." And they did!

Dear Jesus, please give me, too, the excitement of being a fisher of men. Help me to trust that if I, by faith, launch out into the deep, I am guaranteed the prize of seeing new people brought into Your kingdom. Give me the faith I need to forsake all and follow You. Amen.

And That's the Truth!

Read Luke 22:7–20.

> "They ... found everything just as Jesus had said" (Luke 22:13 TLB).

I hope that you will read for yourself the beautiful story found in Luke 22:7–20.

Probably an entire series of meditations could be written about these verses alone! As I prayed about these verses, so familiar and yet so awesome, I was struck by the powerful message of verse 13: "They ... found everything just as Jesus had said."

The Bible is God's Word, as living and applicable to my life today as it was when holy men of God were first inspired to write it down. In this holy Word, I find answers to all of life's hardest questions: Why does the world exist? How does it keep going? Why is there so much sin and evil in the world? Why am I here? Do I really matter? And as I test the claims made by God in His Word, I find that every part of it is true, just as Jesus had said.

Because of this, my life has value. I can trust every promise that Jesus made. I can be victorious even when Satan hurls his lies and accusations in my direction. My faith in God gives me the power to make Satan run off in humiliation, simply by reminding him that Jesus is the Lord of my life. (Read James 4:7.) My sins have been forgiven. I am enjoying an abundant life of blessings on earth, and I'll someday spend eternity with my wonderful Lord in heaven.

If you do not have this same assurance in your heart, "Search the Scriptures" (read John 5:39).

Test God's promises for yourself. Ask God to reveal Himself to you through His Word. You, too, will find everything is just as Jesus has said.

"Lord, I believe; help my unbelief!" (Mark 9:24 RSV).

Topsy-Turvy

Read Luke 22:66 to 23:25.

> "Away with this Man! Release Barabbas to us!" (Luke 23:18 NIV).

From Luke 22:66 to Luke 23:25, there is a great deal of action in the passion story—but everything seems out of focus, bizarre, and upside down:

Jesus appears at His trial—at *dawn* (22:66)!

When Jesus answers their questions honestly, He is *condemned* (22:70–71)!

The accusations dredged up against Him are totally *false*! (Read both Luke 23:2 and Matthew 22:21.)

Pilate and Herod, longtime bitter enemies, become *friends* (23:12)!

And finally, Barabbas, the notorious prisoner, an insurrectionist, robber, and murderer, is released to society—at the people's request (23:25)!

What an exciting story! What twists of plot! How will it all end?

As Christians, we know that this is much more than just a story, even more than the story of Jesus. It is also our story! Each of us is a Barabbas, a condemned sinner, now released! Each of us is the reason that sinless, innocent Jesus walked through these senseless events to His death. Jesus *knew* how it all would end—with His victorious resurrection! So we know, too, how our own stories will end. We have been released from the punishment of sin to the joy of spending eternity with our Savior!

As the joy of this release fills our hearts, it can do nothing less than radiate to the people around us. Love, joy, patience, forgiveness, and all the other gifts of the Spirit can be ours, permeating all of our relationships. Praise God! We have been released!

Dear Jesus, I am so amazed and overwhelmed that You suffered Your crucifixion and death to save *me* from my sins! Thank You, Jesus, with all of my heart. Help me to truly be a witness of Your love and salvation to many other people. In Your wonderful name I pray. Amen.

Always Be Ready!

Read Luke 22:35–38.

As often as I have read Luke chapter 22, I have never focused on only these four verses. Jesus is having an unusual conversation with His disciples!

Yes, He had conversed with them earlier, as see in chapter 21, about the future, including upcoming times of stress and persecution. But as crowds continued to gather at the temple to hear Jesus's teaching, and as the preparation for the Passover was taking place, I can't imagine that the disciples were keeping their focus on the troublesome events of the future.

Jesus had just told Peter that he, Peter, would one day deny having ever known Jesus. What kind of a prediction was that? Peter, who loved Jesus so much, couldn't begin to comprehend it!

Then Jesus reminded the disciples of how well things had gone in the past as they had preached the Good News of Jesus. So now what was Jesus talking about, telling them to be well prepared with a duffel bag, clothes, money—and even a couple of swords! How confusing! What was Jesus expecting to happen in the future?

As I have pondered these verses, I have begun to realize that even though my life is blessed with income, food, a lovely home, and many other joyful blessings, I, too, live in a sinful world, and things can change! If that ever happens to me, will I lose my faith? No, I will not! Because the Bible, God's Word, has taught me about His love and salvation, so I can cling to that even when things change.

In verse 37, Jesus stated, "Everything written about Me by the prophets will come true" (TLB). Those words didn't refer only to His crucifixion; they also pointed ahead to His resurrection and that Jesus would return to heaven to prepare a place for each of us—for eternity—no matter what happens while we are on earth.

Dear Jesus, thank You for coming to earth and living as a person, dying for my sins, and giving me the promise of eternal salvation. Help me to *always* trust Your Word! Amen.

The Death of Two Thieves

Read Luke 23:1–43.

> "I tell you the truth; today you will be with Me in Paradise!" (Luke 23:43 NIV).

When Jesus was crucified, He was executed with two thieves whose crimes were so severe as to merit crucifixion. Each of these malefactors was well aware of his own guilt and misdeeds. There they hung on crosses, one on Jesus's right side, the other on His left side. Each man suffered excruciating pain that would lead to certain death.

One of the thieves clung tenaciously to his guilt and sins. Even while suffering indescribable pain, he managed to taunt Jesus with scathing words.

The other thief, however, began to see that he was suspended only inches from the one who proclaimed Himself to be the Door of Life. This thief was well aware of his own guilt; he knew he was paying a just punishment for his sins.

But this thief began to realize that his punishment did not have to end in *eternal* death, even though his earthly death was imminent. Through his dying pain, he reached out to Jesus in the only way he could, by calling out to Him, "Jesus, remember me when You come into Your kingdom!"

And, oh! The joy that flooded his very soul as he heard Jesus reply, "Today you will be with Me in paradise!"

There was no release from earthly pain, no last-minute reprieve of his torturous death, no change in his past or present life. But what an eternal change resulted in his soul!

Two thieves, equally guilty, were given the opportunity to open the Door of Life and enter eternal rest, with full pardon for all of their sins. And this gift is also *ours*, just for the asking.

It was given to a thief hanging on a cross, and it is offered to each one of us. We simply need to pray to Jesus and ask for it!

The following is a sinner's prayer. It is yours to pray, if it is the sincere desire of your heart:

"Jesus, I know that I am a sinner and that I deserve eternal punishment for my sins. But You have offered me eternal salvation through Your death and resurrection. I want this gift of love from You. Please forgive me and accept me as Your perfect child. Thank You! Amen."

A Very Personal Bible Study

Read Luke 24:13–53. Then focus on verse 32: "They asked each other, 'Were not our hearts burning within us while He talked with us on the road and opened the Scriptures to us?'" (NIV).

Have you ever experienced a great disappointment that left you wondering if all of the energy and enthusiasm you devoted to a project had been in vain? I'm sure that is how Cleopas and his friend felt as they began their seven-mile walk to Emmaus.

Their hearts were heavy as they reviewed the horrifying and unexpected way that the life of Jesus had ended. Rather than being their long-awaited Messiah, He had been condemned and crucified! He was dead!

A man joined their walk and surprised them by calling them "Foolish!" *We* know that this man was Jesus; however, Cleopas and his friend were kept by God from recognizing Him. But through God's Word, as this man explained scripture passages from Genesis through the Prophets, He rekindled and encouraged their faith.

I have always loved this story! How exciting it must have been to hear Jesus's own voice explain the mysteries of the Bible! But why didn't He reveal Himself right away to the two men as they walked and talked? I think Jesus wanted them to learn that He can be seen *through His Word* and that God's Word is *always* true.

This story is a lesson for us all: God's Word *is* the voice of Jesus, and it reveals His love and faithfulness to each of us. The more we read and study the Bible, the more Jesus personally reveals

Himself to us. Through His Word, we can grow closer to Him and then reflect Him to the sinful world.

When Cleopas and his friend finally recognized Jesus, their grief was overcome with joy! They immediately and excitedly walked seven miles back to Jerusalem to share their excitement with fellow Christians. With the support of the church, we, too, can share our sorrows and joys, and through His Word, we can each grow in our own personal relationship with Jesus. What a blessing!

Dear Jesus, thank You for Your personal love and faithfulness for me. Please help me to grow even closer to You as I study Your Word. Amen.

"Go and Sin No More!"

Read John 8:1–11. Then focus on verse 11: "'Neither do I condemn you,' Jesus declared. 'Go now and leave your life of sin'" (NIV).

Have you ever been caught in a sin?

Think back over your life. Perhaps your mother caught you writing on a wall with her lipstick. Perhaps your teacher caught you copying someone else's answers. Perhaps your boss caught you playing a game instead of using your computer for your work. In any of those instances, were your peers aware of your misdeed?

In John 8:1–11, we read the familiar story of the woman caught in adultery and brought before Jesus. Only a short time before, a man had been causing her to feel desirable and valued. Now she was shamed and accused before a whole group of men, as well as church leaders, Jesus, and anyone else who was around to witness her humiliation. What punishment would she have to endure?

Isaiah must have felt as she did when he exclaimed in despair, "Woe to me! I am ruined! For I am a man of unclean lips, and I live among a people of unclean lips!" (Isaiah 6:5 NIV). God's answer to him, as He purged Isaiah's mouth with a live coal, was "See, this has touched your lips; your guilt is taken away and your sin is atoned for" (6:7).

Jesus did not subject the adulterous woman to physical punishment. He knew that before long, He, Himself, would bear that punishment in her place. He simply stated, "Neither do I condemn you; go now and leave your life of sin" (John 8:11 NIV).

Oh, the blessed relief! The unbelievable awareness of freedom, salvation, and renewal! The adulterous woman had been forgiven and given a fresh start! But could she really give up her habitual, sinful ways? Look back on your own life. Have you been able, with Jesus's help, to give up some sinful habits? If so, how has this been possible for you to do?

Jesus, Himself, gives us the answer: "Most assuredly, I say to you, whoever sins is a slave to sin. Now a slave has no permanent place in the family; but a son belongs to it forever. So if the Son sets you free, you will be free indeed" (John 8:34–36 NIV).

And the best news is that when Jesus returns to take us to heaven, we will be raised *imperishable*, never to experience the fear, shame, and sorrow of sin (1 Corinthians 15:52)!

Dear God, "Thanks be to You, Who gives us the victory through our Lord Jesus Christ!" Amen.

(1 Corinthians 15:57 NIV)

The Fall of the Evil Prince

Jesus said, "Now is the time for judgement on this world;
now the prince of this world will be driven out."
—John 12:31 (NIV)

Well before the creation of time, a cataclysmic event occurred in eternity. Some of this story is revealed in Ezekiel 28, which is actually the story of Lucifer. He was a dazzling angel, created in perfection, with a voice like music and an appearance as brilliant as precious gems. He was the anointed guardian angel, above all the others. But Lucifer's position and beauty corrupted him with pride. Isaiah 14:12–14 reveals five of his pride statements, concluding with, "I will be like the Most High!"

No! The Most High God banished Lucifer and his followers, one-third of the angelic host, to hell—ultimately the place of judgment and "eternal fire prepared for the devil and his angels" (Matthew 25:41).

The story of this battle is the thread throughout the scriptures. Many times, Lucifer (Satan) has felt victorious. When Cain killed Abel, Satan thought he'd eliminated the promised savior. He again thought he'd been victorious when Abraham lifted the knife to sacrifice Isaac. When the great King Xerxes flippantly agreed with Haman to wipe out all the Jews, Satan was fully confirmed of victory. But no! The Most High God continually had the perfect plan!

When the time was right, God's Son Himself entered the world. To Satan, he appeared as a helpless infant. Satan planned to snuff out the baby's life through the power of King Herod. Once again, his plan was foiled! Later, when Jesus, as an adult, confronted

Satan's demons to cast them out of possessed humans, those fallen angels recoiled in horror and begged Jesus to leave them alone, because they knew where they would end up—in hell! (Read Luke 8:26–33.)

So Satan acted through Judas, the Sanhedrin, and even Pontius Pilate to do away with the God/man. Ha! Ha! Jesus was crucified! At last, Lucifer won! How his cold eyes must have blazed with arrogance as Jesus descended into hell!

But Jesus descended to the depths of hell only to claim victory! And then He rose! Satan was now eternally defeated. And God's victory is shared with each of us who believe on Jesus's name.

Dear Lord, thank You for eternally being in control of Your perfect plan for the salvation of humankind. Help me to trust You with Your plan for *my* life. In the name of Your precious Son, Jesus. Amen.

What Is Jesus Saying?

Read John 16:7–20.

> "But I tell you the truth: It is for your good that I am going away. Unless I go away, the Counselor will not come to you; but if I go, I will send him to you" (John 16:7). "I tell you the truth: you will weep and mourn while the world rejoices. You will grieve, but your grief will turn to joy!" (John 16:20 NIV).

The following could be the thoughts of someone who lived at the time of Jesus:

I love Jesus so much, and we have been through so much together. My heart had never been as light and joyous as when I was with Jesus. We grew so close as I spent my days with Him. I felt my knowledge and understanding expand as I grew in heart, mind, soul, and spirit.

Then came those terrible, dark days when Jesus was arrested, put on trial, convicted, and crucified. It all happened so fast, and it was all so wrong! I have never suffered such grief and despair as when I saw my beloved Jesus's broken body hanging dead on the cross. Oh, why couldn't I be dead too? How could I possibly go on with my life? What was life without Jesus?

The worst part was all of my doubts. I had trusted Him to be my Savior. I thought I could believe everything He said. Had I been wrong? Had He betrayed me? I was in such turmoil with my confusion.

And then—who can explain this?—at my darkest moment, here He is! Alive again! With me! The same as before, only even better: glorified, eternal, never to die again, to walk with me forever! All of His promises seem to have been true. I have begun to relax and trust Him; once more, my heart is filled with lightness and joy.

But now—what is Jesus saying? He is going away again—and it is for my *good*?

Through my tears, I listen carefully to all of His words. I now know that I can trust Jesus implicitly every time He says, "I tell you the truth." Jesus is saying that He won't leave me alone to grieve; He will send me a Comforter, the very Spirit of truth. And Jesus also promises that He, Himself, will see me again! This fills me with joy that no one can take away.

How often Jesus has assured me with those wonderful words, "I tell you the truth." I will review those blessed statements and hide them in my heart. When Satan, the prince of this world, tries to convict me of guilt, I will know that he now stands condemned.

My grief has turned to joy! I have my Jesus, and He tells me the truth!

Soli Deo Gloria

Blood and Water

Read John 19:33–37.

> Instead, one of the soldiers pierced Jesus' side with a spear, bringing a sudden flow of blood and water. (John 19:34 NIV)

The Jewish leaders were running out of time! The next day was not only a Sabbath day, it was also a celebration of Passover. There were still things to be done in preparation, including the slaying of paschal lambs. How could the leaders handle all of this while the criminals were still alive, hanging on their crosses? Jesus was one of those crucified men. Perhaps those men would die more quickly if their legs were whacked and broken. Can you imagine the horror, sorrow, and emotion that John, Jesus's beloved disciple, felt as he witnessed all of this?

Soldiers came and broke the legs of the two criminals who had been crucified with Jesus, but Jesus, the true Paschal Lamb, had already died, so He was not struck. This fulfilled the prophecy found in Psalm 34:19–20: "A righteous man may have many troubles, but the Lord delivers him from them all. He protects all his bones; not one of them will be broken" (NIV).

To prove that Jesus had died, His side was pierced with a spear. Blood and water flowed out, proving that yes, He was dead, and also becoming symbols for Christians of the blessings of baptism and holy communion, the forgiveness of our sins.

As my husband, Bruce, and I raised our three children, we witnessed plenty of blood. One child's hand, for example, broke through a window; another child was viciously bitten by a dog;

another child's leg was bloodied and broken when on a snowy day he decided to sled down from our garage roof! With farm relatives, I also witnessed the heads chopped off of chickens while blood spewed into the air! Yes, I've seen plenty of blood—perhaps you have too—but never both blood *and* water.

What then does John 19:34 reveal to us?

John, who wrote these verses, adds further comments in 1 John 5:6–8. Jesus's water and blood are witnesses of both His baptism and His death. His water also reminds us of our own baptism, and His blood is even now a part of our communion. Jesus Himself described the communion wine as His own blood (read Mark 14:23–24). So the appearance of both Jesus's blood and water, when the soldier pierced His side, gives each of us a personal connection to His sacrificial death on our behalf. It also shows that, as a human, Jesus truly died.

I like to remember that one of the criminals who was crucified and had his legs broken, enduring so much pain and punishment, also came to faith in Jesus as he hung on the cross. And Jesus assured him that once he died, he would live again, with Jesus, in heaven for all eternity! That story is found in Luke 23:40–43.

We can be very grateful that John witnessed Jesus's death and wrote about it for our salvation. God's wonderful Word, the Bible, allows each of us to meet Jesus. It teaches that, without a doubt, Jesus is both part of the Triune God and a human being. His water and blood offer the promise of eternal salvation to every person who believes this. When we attend Sunday services and experience the support of a church, we can then live as disciples and encourage others to meet Jesus and come to faith. What a wonderful blessing!

Dear Jesus, thank You for all of the blessings You have given to me, but most of all, that You washed away my sins and saved me with Your precious blood. Help me to be a faithful witness of Your life, so that others may also be drawn to the blessings of Your salvation. Amen.

All in His Time

Jesus said to them, "It is not for you to know the times of seasons which the Father has put in His own authority."
—Acts 1:7 (NKJV)

"Dear Lord, if You would just give me a clue about how this will all end, it would be so much easier for me to make my plans!"

Have you ever approached the Lord with such a prayer? The disciples inquired of Jesus in just that way. "If only You would explain to us how Your kingdom will be established," they pleaded, "we will be better equipped to serve You!" But Jesus did not reveal the details, which, in fact, were known only to the Father. And His Father—their Father too—knew that the disciples could not bear to know everything that was to transpire. In His love, He simply asked them to trust Him for power.

In her book *The Hiding Place*, Corrie ten Boom relates a story from her own young life that can help us to understand this kind of answer from God. As she rode on a train with her father, she suddenly asked him about something that was much too mature for her to understand. She writes:

> [My father] turned to look at me, as he always did when answering a question, but to my surprise he said nothing. At last he stood up, lifted his traveling case from the rack over our heads, and set it on the floor.
>
> "Will you carry it off the train, Corrie?" he asked.
>
> I stood up and tugged at it. It was crammed with the watches and spare parts he had purchased that morning.

"It's too heavy," I said.

"Yes," he said. "And it would be a pretty poor father who would ask his little girls to carry such a load. It's the same way, Corrie, with knowledge. Some knowledge is too heavy for children. When you are older and stronger you can bear it. For now you must trust me to carry it for you."

And I was satisfied. More than satisfied—wonderfully at peace. There were answers to this and all my hard questions—for now I was content to leave them in my father's keeping.

Dear Father, help me to trust You with the perfect plan You have for my life. You have the answers to all my hard questions. Let me be content to leave them in Your keeping Amen.

God tells us in His Word: "A man's heart plans his way, but the Lord directs his steps"

(Proverbs 16:9 NKJV).

An Amazingly Wonderful Body Part

Read Romans 12:6–21.

> "Just as there are many parts to our bodies, so it is with Christ's body. We are all parts of it, and it takes every one of us to make it complete, for we each have different work to do" (verses 4 and 5 TLB).

If you could choose to be a body part, what would you choose to be? A heart? A stomach? A strong arm muscle? A brain? Would you consider being an intestine, or a fingernail, or simply a hair? I'm sure we all think of some parts as being more important and indispensable than others. But each and every part of our bodies contributes to who we are as a whole person.

Think about it. When something happens to damage and cause pain to a part of your body—whether a large and important or seemingly insignificant part—your entire body reacts. Has anyone ever pulled your hair? That hurts! Have you ever lost a fingernail? I have. When my son David was an infant, I sliced through my thumbnail with a can opener and ended up with four stitches in it. Ow! Besides the pain, there was the great aggravation of keeping my bandaged thumb dry for several days. In addition, since David continually saw my thumb as a banana, I had to somehow keep it from his reach. Believe me, that thumbnail became as important to me as any other body part!

God describes His church as being one body, with Christ as the head. Each one of us plays a unique role in that body, whether we see ourselves as important or unimportant. God sees each one of us as a significant part of the whole!

I don't need to wonder whether I am a major organ or simply a toe. I only need to be what I am, whether a finger, an eye, a bone, an inner organ, a healthy blood cell, or a piece of skin, and that's how Christ will use me as a part of His wonderful body. What happens when one body part stops working? The entire body becomes affected. And that's what happens to Christ's body if a believer ceases to be a productive part of God's church.

Bench warmers, or people who attend church but do nothing else to support it, are artificial body parts. We each need to contribute to the church in terms of time, talent, and treasure. The Bible speaks of this as producing fruit. Jesus condemned what seemed to be a perfectly healthy fig tree—tall, filled with leaves, providing shade from oppressing heat—simply because it did not produce fruit. (Read Mark 11:13–14.) Romans 12:6–21 gives us many specific examples of the type of fruit that Jesus wants us to bear. When we live this way, we are each a contributing, healthy part of Christ's body, nurtured by God's perfect love.

Dear Lord, thank You for accepting me as a part of your Son's perfect body! Amen.

Sitting with My Heavenly Dad

> God is so rich in mercy; He loved us so much that even
> though we were spiritually dead and doomed by our sins,
> He gave us back our lives again when He raised Christ
> from the dead ... and lifted us up from the grave unto
> glory along with Christ, where we sit with Him in the
> heavenly realms—all because of what Christ Jesus did.
> —Ephesians 2:4–6 (TLB)

My father, Norman, died several years ago at age ninety-six. He had been a lifetime member of our Lutheran church, having also attended the Lutheran grade school and becoming an extremely active member of the church congregation, where he served twice as president. Norman was a violinist and a singer. He had a marvelous sense of humor, he was an incredibly gifted artist, and he served the Lord all of his life. I learned so much from my father, and he and I had a close, loving relationship.

As much as I miss my earthly dad, through the past years, I have grown closer and closer to God the Father, my heavenly Dad. The following Bible verses are a joyful encouragement to me:

> When I think of the wisdom and scope of His plan I
> fall down on my knees and pray to the Father of all the
> great family of God—some of them already in heaven
> and some down here on earth—that out of His glorious,
> unlimited resources He will give you the mighty inner
> strengthening of His Holy Spirit. (Ephesians 3:15–16
> TLB)

My earthly father is no longer a part of my sinful world. But I am—and if you are reading this, so are you. And no matter what your family life has been, God the Father is *your* heavenly Dad too. He created you, and He loves you with His powerful, everlasting love. He sacrificed His only Son, Jesus, to save you from sin and give you the promise of eternity with all of His family. Let this be a joy in your life as it is in mine!

Dear heavenly Dad, thank You for creating me and for saving me from my sinful life through the sacrifice of You Son, Jesus. With the aid of Your Holy spirit, help me to use my life as a joyful witness of You to the sinful world. I am so looking forward to meeting You in person when I enter heaven! Amen.

Gratitude for Those Who Prayed for and Witnessed to My Soul

I pray that you may be active in sharing your
faith, so that you will have a full understanding
of every good thing we have in Christ.
—Philemon, verse 6 (NIV)

For many years, as I would read the opening paragraph of this sincere and personal letter that Paul, who was in prison for being a Christian, wrote to Philemon, my heart would overflow with gratitude and praise for all the Christian people the Lord has placed in my life: my parents and early teachers who taught me of Jesus and the plan of salvation; Bible study leaders, pastors, friends, and family members with strong faith who have prayed for me and encouraged my faith; my church, which preaches the true Word; books, music, and Christian radio, which have continued to teach me and help me walk closely with the Lord.

Sometimes I have wondered why my life has been so blessed. I was placed by God into a Christian family; I attended a Christian grade school; I live in a Christian community and in a country where I am free to worship. Why *shouldn't* I be filled with gratitude? It seems that my faith has been so easily handed to me.

In more recent years, as I thank God for the faith that I have in common with others, God has also filled my heart with a great appreciation for the faith I see in people with whom I seem to have little in common. I thank Him in prayer for people around the world who are severely persecuted for their faith but do not lose their faith, and I also thank God for the people He has put directly in my path who show unwavering faith despite great personal hardships: a troubled single mom; a handicapped couple who face tremendous struggles with society; a very low-income woman who still puts God first with her tithes and prayers. I am humbled as I thank God for their tremendous witness to me and for their faithfulness to Him. As I beseech His blessings on their behalf, my heart overflows with gratitude and praise!

O Lord, I am so overwhelmed with gratitude that I am a part of Your family! Let me never think that I am more deserving than any other person of all the wonderful blessings You have showered upon me. Please help me to always be sensitive to the world around me and its many unsaved souls. Let the words of my mouth and the meditation of my heart be always ready to share Your love and Your wonderful plan of salvation with people You put in my path. In the name of Your precious Son, Jesus, I pray. Amen.

Worry-Free!

Cast all your anxiety on Him because He cares for you!
—1 Peter 5:7 (NIV)

A woman wrote to Dear Abby, complaining that a college friend regularly phones her to air the same vague worries over and over again. She has understandably grown tired of being a sounding board for someone who refuses to accept her advice.

Thankfully, God never gets tired of listening to us. He wants us to share everything with Him, including the things that cause us to worry. More than that, He urges us to bring our problems to Him so that He can dispose of them in His own way, once and for all, and free us from the stress they bring.

We need to keep in mind that our Lord has not promised to solve all our problems just the way we might want. The disease may not be cured; the money may not come. Before He went to the cross to die for the sins of the world, Jesus prayed, "Father, if You are willing, take this cup from Me; yet not My will, but Yours be done" (Luke 22:42 NIV).

Like Jesus, we need to humble ourselves before our Father's will, accepting whatever His love brings us. He promises to take our worries and lovingly care and provide for us in every circumstance of our lives.

Now read 1 Peter 5:10. It lets us know that while we are living on earth, we may endure suffering. But God's Word promises that, when we leave this world and enter eternal life with Him, God, our heavenly Father, will restore, establish, and strengthen us for eternity through the eternal glory of Christ. What a beautiful and encouraging promise!

I am Yours for time and eternity, dear Lord. Enable me to do Your work unhampered by anxiety or fear. In the name of Your precious Son, Jesus, I pray. Amen.

For Yours is the Kingdom and the Power and the Glory Forever! Amen.

After this I heard what sounded like the roar of a great multitude in heaven shouting, "Halleluia! Salvation and glory and power belong to our God, for true and just are His judgements. He has condemned the great prostitute who corrupted the earth by her adulteries. He has avenged on her the blood of His servants." And again they shouted, "Halleluia! The smoke from her goes up forever and ever." The twenty-four elders and the four living creatures fell down and worshiped God, Who was seated on the throne. And they cried, "Amen, Halleluia!" Then a voice came from the throne saying, "Praise our God, all you His servants, you who fear Him, both small and great!" Then I heard what sounded like a great multitude, like the roar of rushing waters and like loud peals of thunder, shouting, "Halleluia! For our Lord God Almighty reigns. Let us rejoice and be glad and give Him glory! For the wedding of the Lamb has come, and His bride has made herself ready. Fine linen, bright and clean, was given to her to wear." ("Fine linen" stands for the righteous acts of the saints.)
—Revelation 19:1–8 (NIV)

As I ponder these verses from Revelation, I begin to imagine watching a scene similar to the opening Parade of Nations, of our televised Olympics. In my mind, I picture people of every kindred, tribe, and nation on earth, waiting to enter the arena, their clothes dazzling white, their faces shining. Then I think about the archangels Michael and Gabriel, and I imagine some of the comments they might be making as they observe this great event.

"Look, Gabriel, there's Lucinda Smith! She was brought to faith, you may remember, by Ellen Brown, as they waited in line at the grocery store."

"I remember well, Michael, and I know Ellen will be thrilled and surprised to see Lucinda enter the arena!"

"Michael, here come all the believers who were brought to faith by the *Lutheran Hour* and other Christian radio broadcasts."

"What a crowd, Gabriel! Look, here come the Spanish believers who came to faith as a result of a big mission project!"

"Yes, Michael, the prayers of many believers helped to make that project a big success! Oh, look! The next crowd of African believers came to faith as a result of the $400,000 that was raised to support the missionaries who were sent to Ghana. What a thrill to see them enter the arena!"

Soon, all of the earth's believers have entered. Not a single person from all time has been forgotten. All of the martyrs stand together. They are joined by the cherubim, the seraphim, all the angels, and finally the archangels.

An excited, expectant hush falls over the throng. Then the clear, beautiful voice of angel Gabriel fills the arena:

"And now ... originally from the Celestial City but more recently hailing from Earth itself ... our Lord and Earth's Savior ... Jesus Christ!"

Then Jesus appears, not in a spotlight because He, Himself, is the source of light. The roar of approval, excitement, and adoration that rises from the crowd is like nothing that was ever heard at a winning White Sox baseball game, more like the sound of rushing waters and loud peals of thunder. All of earth's believers in salvation through Christ and all of heaven's hosts can at last fully look upon the face of God. They have all of eternity to share their stories of faith with the angels and with one another. And they will live forever with Jesus, to whom belongs the kingdom and the power and the glory forever! Amen!

> Oh, that with yonder sacred throng
> We at His feet may fall!
> We'll join the everlasting song
> And crown Him Lord of all!
> And crown Him Lord of all!
> (Verse 7 of the hymn "All Hail the Power of Jesus's Name,"
> written in 1779 by Edward Peronet)

This poem is based on both Old and New Testament Bible stories

Trust Him and Obey

The Lord God said to Jonah, "Here's something you must do:
Go preach to all the Ninevites. I want to save them too."
But Jonah didn't like the plan; he tried to hide from God and ran.
So God used a great whale to help old Jonah understand
That when God says to you, "Here's something you must do,"
He'll show you the way; so trust Him and obey. (Read Jonah chapters 1–3.)

Young David was a shepherd who loved and served the Lord.
Goliath was a giant man who could not be ignored.
Dave slung a stone, and by God's might, the giant fell without a fight.
Then David cut Goliath's head off with the giant's sword.
So when God says to you, "Here's something you must do,"
He'll show you the way; so trust Him and obey. (Read 1 Samuel chapter 17.)

Up in an open window, where everyone could see,
Bold Daniel prayed three times a day, despite the king's decree.
When thrown into the lions' den, he thought he would be eaten! Then
God's angel closed the lions' mouths, and Daniel was set free.
So when God says to you, "Here's something you must do,"
He'll show you the way; so trust Him and obey. (Read Daniel chapter 6.)

While shackled in a prison with security so tight,
Silas and Paul sang psalms of praise and prayed with all their might.
At midnight, with a mighty roar, an earthquake broke the prison door!
The jailer and his family were baptized that very night.
So when God says to you, "Here's something you must do,"
He'll show you the way; so trust Him and obey. (Read Acts chapter 16.)

The women carried spices on that first Easter day.
They wished to anoint Jesus, as in the tomb He lay.
But while their hearts were filled with gloom—how would they get inside the tomb?—
God sent a mighty angel to roll the stone away!
So when God says to you, "Here's something you must do,"
He'll show you the way; so trust Him and obey. (Read Matthew 28:1–10.)

And sometimes if it seems to you that God's will is too hard to do,
Then read the Bible stories; they will help you understand
That when God says to you, "Here's something you must do,"
He'll show you the way; so trust Him and obey!

On a Pathway through Some Psalms

The LORD watches over the way of the righteous;
but the way of the wicked shall perish.
—Psalm 1:6 (NIV)

This Bible verse lets us know that there are only two roads that lead to eternity. The word *way*, in the original Hebrew, *derek*, means "road." There is only *one* road leading to heaven: "the way of righteousness." The other road, the way of the ungodly, leads *only* to hell. Jesus said, "I AM the Way, and the Truth, and the Life, and no one comes to the Father but by Me" (John 14:6 NIV). And Isaiah tells us, in chapter 30:21, "This is the Way; walk in it" (NIV).

The Bible has some encouraging statements concerning our *walk* with the LORD:

1. In Genesis 17:1 (NIV), God said to Abraham, "I AM God Almighty; walk before Me and be blameless."

2. Isaiah 40:31 (TLB) tells us that "They that wait upon the LORD shall renew their strength; they shall mount up with wings like eagles; thy shall run and not be weary; they shall walk and not faint."

3. Second Corinthians 5:7 (RSV) reminds us that "we walk by faith not by sight."

4. In Galatians 5:16 (RSV), we are reminded to "walk by the Spirit, and do not gratify the desires of the flesh."

5. First John 1:6 (NKJV) is very encouraging, as it tells that "if we walk in the Light, as He is in the Light, we have fellowship with one another; and the blood of Jesus, His Son, cleanses us from all sin."

6. The Bible also tell us things about our *feet*. Here are a few of the many verses on that subject:

Second Samuel 22:37 (NKJV): "You enlarged my path under me, so my feet did not slip."
Romans 10:15 (TLB): "How beautiful are the feet of those who preach the Gospel of peace."
Ephesians 6:15 (TLB): "Wear shoes that are able to speed you as you preach the Good News of peace with God."

These Bible verses, along with many others, can greatly encourage us as we enjoy hiking on a pathway through some psalms.

Dear LORD, Please be with me as I follow a pathway through some of the psalms that are included in the book of Your Word. Help me to grow closer to You every day as I read them and learn more about You through them. In Jesus's name I pray. Amen.

On a Pathway through Some Psalms

Your Word is a Lamp to my feet and a Light to my path.
—Psalm 119:105 (NKJV)

The Bible's book of 150 psalms, which is both a prayer book and a song book, was written mostly by David, a shepherd who became a king when chosen and anointed by God. But other authors are also mentioned: Asaph, who wrote Psalm 50 and Psalms 73–83; Solomon, who wrote Psalms 72 and 127; Heman, who wrote Psalm 88; Ethan, who wrote Psalm 89; and Moses, who wrote Psalm 90.

As you begin to follow the pathway through some of the psalms, remember to thank God for being the lamp to your feet and the light to your path!

Psalm 1—Growing Like a Tree

The first psalm from the total group of 150 psalms is like a gateway into the treasure house of communion with God. Verse 1 states that "Blessed is the man" who enters into this path of righteousness, eager to walk in delight with the LORD. Read verses 1–3.

To be "blessed," an expression which shows up many times throughout the book of Psalms, is to reserve happiness in our hearts from God's forgiving mercy. Read Psalm 32:1. The happiness grows out of being totally committed to God. Read Psalm 84:12. We are also blessed during times of conflict and stress. Read Psalm 94:12–15.

And what does it mean to meditate day and night on God's law? Read Genesis 1:26–31 and 2:15–17. From the early beginning, both Adam and Eve gave in to the temptation from Satan, the serpent, and thus gave in to sin. Read Genesis 3:1–7. But even though their sin made God very angry, He gave them the promise of salvation. Read Genesis 3:14–15. Then read Romans 5:12–21. The promise of salvation through God's Son, Jesus, is what allows us to feel blessed! And the more time we spend meditating on God's Word, the more we will grow in our faith.

Verse 3 of Psalm 1 compares us, as we grow in our faith, to a growing tree that also produces fruit. Read that verse. This is mentioned again in Jeremiah 17:7 and also in Psalm 82:12–14. Read each of those verses too. Aren't these words encouraging to us as we grow in our faith?

Now read verses 4–6 of Psalm 1. People who ignore God's Word are "the wicked," eventually to be driven away by God for eternity, having forfeited God's blessings of forgiveness and salvation. But the people who have dedicated their faith and trust to the LORD will be saved. What a beautiful note of assurance for all who believe!

Dear LORD, as I look around me and view Your amazing creation, help me to grow in my love and service to You, just as a tree does when it grows and produces fruit. In Jesus's name. Amen.

On a Pathway through Some Psalms: Psalm 23—A Psalm of David

Read the twenty-third psalm.

It is interesting to note that in verses 1–3, the pronouns are in the third person. But beginning with verse 4, the psalmist, David, talks directly to the Lord, and now the pronouns are in the second person. The darkness that is passing through causes him to talk directly *to* the Lord instead of just *about* the Lord.

As my Shepherd and I travel along, I may at times leave the path or lag behind. He loves me too much to allow me to get lost or injure myself, so He corrects me with His rod and staff. Read Hebrews 12:5–11. The rod and staff are both my protection and correction.

What could be the purpose of dark days in my life? Read Hosea 5:15–6:1.

How do dark days and sorrow benefit a person? Read these and record your thoughts:

Read Psalm 50:15.
Read Psalm 119:49–50.
Read Psalm 119:67 and 71.
Read Hebrews 12:10–11.
Read John 15:2.
Read 1 Peter 2:20.

Now read Psalm 23:5. Here the scene changes from a pasture to a banquet hall. God is seen as more than only a Shepherd; He is also a King who bountifully lavishes all of His rich provisions on

His guests. In one of Jesus's parables, He spoke of a feast in the kingdom of God. Read about that in Luke 14:15–24.

Next, read Revelation 19:9. Here an angel speaks of people who will be invited to a heavenly wedding feast. Then return to Psalm 23:5. Here, the psalmist David speaks of being a guest of honor in God's house. Enemies can only look on helplessly while the guest enjoys the security of God's home. This reminds us of an Oriental custom, seen at times in some of Jesus's stories, which allows onlookers to observe a banquet from the outside, not being invited in.

The way that early Oriental people honored their guests was to anoint them with perfumed oil. In scripture, the oil represents the Holy Spirit. In this psalm, anointing with oil represents the Spirit of God controlling my mind, so that evil has no chance to spoil my life.

Read Psalm 23:6. The summary of the psalm assures each of us, as believers, that God's love will be with us as long as we live. Fellowship with God is the climax of all the blessings that human beings can enjoy!

The reason that this short psalm is so helpful is that it reveals to us that Christ meets all the needs of our lives: rest, work, comfort, strength in times of trouble, and our future security. We cannot exhaust the deep message contained in this writing, nor can we improve upon its quiet, comforting beauty.

Remember that there are two important characteristics of this twenty-third psalm:

1. There are no requests from God revealed to us in this psalm.
2. This psalm, even though it is an Old Testament writing, centers our attention upon Christ.

Dear Lord, thank You for inspiring David to write such a beautiful psalm. I look forward to learning more about You through Your Word and someday living with You for eternity! Amen.

On a Pathway through Some Psalms: Psalm 40—A Christlike Attitude

Read Psalm 40. It is a song of praise to God. As you have seen with other psalms, it was written by David about his own experience, but it has a fuller meaning when applied to Christ.

Read verses 1–3 of Psalm 40, and then complete the following sentences:

If I
God will
The result will be that others

This psalm begins with the experience of answered prayer. Notice that it was the Lord for whom David waited, not for men. The Bible has much to say about prayerfully waiting for the Lord's help.

What is the promise in each of the following verses for those who keep looking to the Lord? Read verse 1 again. Those who wait on God are
Read Isaiah 30:18. Those who trust in the Lord are
Read Isaiah 40:31. Those who trust in the Lord shall

We know that God will hear when we cry to Him for help, because His Word gives us that promise from Him. Read Psalm 50:15, Proverbs 15:26, Jeremiah 33:3, and Romans 10:10–13.

Now read Psalm 40:2. The dangerous pit, or quicksand, is a symbol of sin and eternal death. Jesus Himself was delivered from this by God, and it gives us the picture of resurrection. God is the rock or foundation that we are safely set upon. Read both Deuteronomy 32:3–4 and 1 Samuel 2:2.

Now read Psalm 40:3. This new song is a song of praise to God. We each have a new song—one that has never been sung by anyone else. It is our personal song about our deliverance, our resurrection to new life, and our victory over sin and death. When we praise God and let our lives be a reflection of Jesus, others hear our praise and learn how to put their trust in the Lord.

Now read Psalm 4:4. This is the theme of the new song—the wonderful things that God does for us. The worship of the Living God results in joy and praise. Those who worship money, possessions, fame, or other personal prides will eventually have only sorrow before them. God may give us these things, but they are not to be worshipped.

Now read Psalm 40:5. God does many good things for all of His creation; the sun shines on everyone, good and bad alike. However, this verse goes on to say that the Lord has not only done great things for us; He has thought much about us and has planned for us, giving each of us His personal attention. Now take the time to write down ten things God has done just for you, ways that He has blessed you.

Now read Psalm 40:6. This verse speaks of sacrifices, a practice that was done away with when Jesus became the complete and perfect sacrifice for all time and for all humankind. All of the sacrifices of the Old Testament were to illustrate the fact that

God would one day provide an innocent substitute who would die in our place and pay the penalty for our sins. Verse 6 means that God does not want us to sin. He did not want people to continually bring sacrifices for sin; what pleases God is our *obedience*.

Now read verses 7 and 8 of Psalm 40. God prepares our ears to hear Him, and only by God's grace are we able to hear Him and then answer to His call. But only Christ was able to say, as we read in verse 8, "I love to do Your will and I always keep Your teaching in my heart." See John 4:34, where we read that Christ quoted this verse as applying it to Himself. Christ's life was the perfect sacrifice for our sin, making further sin sacrifices unnecessary.

Read Hebrews 10:4–18. The only one who could honestly say Psalm 40:8 was the Lord Jesus Christ.

Now read Psalm 40:9–10. Because of all that the Lord has done for us, we should tell others about Him. David said that he told the Good News that the Lord saves to the meeting of God's people. To whom have you told the Good News of God's salvation?

Read Colossians 4:6. What does it say about how we share the Good News with others?

Now read Psalm 40:11. This verse seems to be a summary statement of all that has preceded it. It is a statement of belief and trust. Will God stop being merciful and loyal to you if you stop being faithful and loyal to Him? What response does God's loving mercy inspire in your heart?

Now read Psalm 40:12–17. Suddenly this psalm has changed to a prayer for help. Many times this is the experience of a godly person. The special blessing and deliverance from God can be followed by a persecution or a new consciousness of sin, or even a time of testing.

Reread verse 12 of Psalm 40. Back in verse 5, David's *blessings* were more than he could count; now we see that his *troubles* are more than he can count. These are not only troubles caused by circumstances beyond his control but troubles that are the result of his own sins. The closer we are to God, the more His light reveals our sins that we may not have noticed before! Thankfully, though the number of someone's sins may be enormous, God's mercies are even more—and they are inexhaustible.

Now reread Psalm 40:13–15. The desperate situation causes David to turn to God in prayer, asking for God's saving power to help him immediately. We may feel that David's words against his enemies are very harsh and could not apply to us, but if we read this while thinking of Satan as our enemy, these verses have even more meaning.

When we think about the last section of Psalm 40 in relation to Christ, we remember the times that God delivered Him from those who wanted to kill Him. Do you remember what happened at the beginning of Jesus's ministry? Read Luke 4:28–30 and John 8:59.

Reread Psalm 40:16. In contrast, David requests that all who trust God should be made glad, joyful, and filled with praise to God.

Also reread verse 17. Again David realizes his own weakness and helplessness. He knows that he is inadequate for the situation before him. But he also knows that God is aware of all the details, and he is assured that God is his Helper and Savior.

Contrast Psalm 40:17 with Revelation 3:17. What is the safest attitude for a Christian to have?

And what does Matthew 5:13 tell us?

The Christlike attitude is an attitude of yielding to God in joyful praise for God's mercy and His promise of salvation. The Christlike attitude that we need is one of completely yielding to God's will and having utter dependence on Him. So now as you enter your week ahead, consider your own attitudes. Are you reflecting Christ to others? With the help of the Holy Spirit, you can!

Dear Lord God, Heavenly Father, thank You for sending Your Son, Jesus, to save me from my sins. Help me to grow closer and closer to You through Your Word. And as I continue to learn more about You through Your Word, please help me to be a reflection of Your love and salvation to people around me. Amen.

On a Pathway through Some Psalms: What Gift Can I Possibly Give?

Read Psalm 50. It was written by Asaph, a man referred to as a "recorder" in 2 Kings 18:18. Here are some of the verses from this psalm:

"The Mighty One, God, the LORD, speaks" (verse 1 NIV).

"He summons the heavens and the earth, that he may judge His people" (verse 4).

"Hear, O my people, and I will speak ... I am God, your God!" (verse 7).

"I do not rebuke you for your sacrifices or your burnt offerings, which are ever before Me. I have no need of a bull from your stall or of goats from your pens" (verses 8–9).

"Every animal of the forest is mine, and the cattle on a thousand hills. I know every bird in the mountains, and the creatures of the field are Mine. If I were hungry, I would not tell you, for the world is Mine, and all that is in it. Do I eat the flesh of bulls, or drink the blood of goats?" (verses 10–13)

Imagine how shocked the Israelites must have been to hear the words from God that are expressed in the above verses. God Himself had commanded the sacrifice of bulls, goats, lambs, grain, incense, and many other things. Their relationship with God totally revolved around sacrifices. So, what did God really want from them?

What God wants us to offer to Him is a sacrifice of *thanksgiving* (verse 14). He is always ready to help us, as He tells us in verse 15: "Call upon Me in the day of trouble; I will deliver you, and You shall honor Me."

Many of us are often faced with the dilemma of gift giving. What gift should I give to the person who really doesn't need anything? Some relatives and friends seem very hard to buy for!

Sometimes the best gift we can give to a friend or relative who needs nothing is our *time*—an invitation to dinner, transportation, help with housework or yardwork, or even a simple visit. This is a gift of love, rather than an item that's returnable with a gift receipt.

God *also* desires our gifts of love. The time, talent, and treasure that we give to Him were also His first gifts to us! More than anything, God wants our response of love. He no longer requires us to sacrifice animals to connect with Him. Psalm 50 goes on to tell us, in verse 14, to "Bring your *thanks* to God as a sacrifice." And with this command comes a beautiful promise:

> Whoever offers thanks as a living sacrifice honors Me.
> I will let everyone who continues in My way see the salvation that comes from God. (Verse 23)

Dear Heavenly Father, I know that Your Son, Jesus, was the Living Sacrifice that You gave to save me from my sins. Please encourage me to grow in thanksgiving for all that You have done for me, so that my very life will be a sacrifice of praise to You! Amen.

On a Pathway through Some Psalms: Psalms 78 and 116—Giving Thanks!

Like Psalm 50, Psalm 78 was also written by Asaph. It gives a recount of Israel's history, pleading with God's people to remember His merciful acts toward them. They are to tell these deeds to their children, so that the children will, in turn, tell them to the next generation.

Sadly, many of our children do not know the great hymns of the faith, even the Christmas carols. And many do not know Bible stories, even the Easter story. And for many, even if they have heard the hymns or the stories, they often do not understand the meaning. Psalm 78 talks about understanding the hidden things. As Charles Spurgeon, a British preacher, author, pastor, and evangelist who lived from 1834 to 1892, wrote, "What is not understood will soon be forgotten."

Read all of Psalm 78 as if it were a story. (A good translation is The Living Bible.)

What do you see as the key lesson of Psalm 78?

It is vital for us to see ourselves in the Israelites, to see how easily we grumble, how easily we forget God's goodness, and how slow we are to find ways to teach of His mercies to the next generation.

Read Psalm 78:1–8. What does the psalmist earnestly desire to share with God's people according to verses 2–4?

With what responsibility are we charged, according to verses 4–6?

As a parent, grandparent, aunt, uncle, or mentor, how are you doing this?

In verses 5–8, find several reasons for passing on the truths of what God has done to the next generation.

Now read Psalm 78:9–16. According to these verses, what are some of the mighty acts of God that the Israelites forgot?

Now read verses 17–20. How did their forgetfulness concerning God's goodness to them impact their hearts?

What is the central meaning and application of the story in these verses? How can you apply it to your own life?

There is a pattern in Psalm 78. Read the verses as mentioned in the following, and then summarize each step in a few words:

Verse 11
Verses 17–20
Verses 21–22
Verses 34–35
Verses 36–37
Verses 38–39

What do you think about the trials you may be facing right now, and how might the past goodness of God help you to face them with faith? Be specific.

Psalm 116 was written by David. What a beautiful picture it gives to us! An awesome God bends down and listens to the humble cry of His child. As He bent down when Hannah cried to Him to be delivered from her barrenness, as He bent down when the Israelites cried to Him to be delivered from their bondage, so God bends down to us when we humbly cry to Him for help. His mercy extends from generation to generation to those who fear Him.

Now read Psalm 116. What stands out to you as you read this psalm?

Some people say that we shouldn't love God because of what He can do for us but that we should simply love Him for who He is. What contrast do you see for that in verse 1?

The psalmist prays with his voice (verse 1). Do you ever pray out loud in your personal prayer time? What advantages can you see for this over silent prayer?

Read verse 2. What impact does answered prayer have upon the psalmist?

What word pictures recall his great need?
What are we to do according to verse 4?
Read verses 5–6. What did the psalmist learn about the Lord from this experience?

What do we learn about the Lord in verses 5–6?

How can you repay the Lord? When God has been good to you, you should share your story with others. In Psalm 116, you can see one clear way to do this, whether you are telling your own story of salvation or another story of deliverance.

Now consider your own story of salvation or a time of deliverance from trouble, when you cried to the Lord for help.

What was your situation?
What did you do?
What did you learn about the Lord?

Now read what the psalmist asks in verse 12.
How does he answer the question in verses 13–14?
What does he further answer in verses 17–19?

These verses from some other psalms may also remind you of a time when God showed mercy to you and delivered you from a problem. Read the verses and ponder them. Then consider sharing your own experiences with another person.

Deliverance from trouble: Psalm 34:4–7
A time of forgiveness: Psalm 51:7
A wonderful deed that God did: Psalm 75:1
Deliverance from death, tears, stumbling: Psalm 116:8
Blessings of harmony with brothers and sisters: Psalm 133

Henry Smith wrote a song in 1978 that summarizes the thoughts of Psalms 78 and 116, which he titled "Give Thanks":

> Give thanks with a grateful heart;
> Give thanks to the Holy One;
> Give thanks, because He's given Jesus Christ, His Son. (repeat)

And now, let the weak say, "I am strong",
Let the poor say, "I am rich
Because of what the Lord has done for us!" (repeat)

Give thanks! Give thanks!

On a Pathway through Some Psalms: Psalm 119 #1—Praise to the Word of God

Psalm 119 is the longest of all of the psalms, with 176 verses. Every verse is praise to the Word of God. The psalm overflows with images from a man who has learned to "hope in God's Word." We learn from him that:

To study God's Word is to find treasure (verse 14).
God's Word is like songs one sings on a long and difficult journey (verse 54).
God's Word is more precious than silver or gold (verse 72).
God's Word is sweeter than honey to his soul (verse 103).
God's Word is a lamp to his feet and a light to his path (verse 105).

Psalm 119 is by far the longest psalm. In Scotland, when George Wishart, bishop of Edinburgh, was facing execution, he availed himself of the custom of the times to have a psalm sung before he, the condemned person, was dropped from the scaffold. Shrewdly, he chose Psalm 119, and pardon arrived before two-thirds of the psalm verses had been sung!

The mechanics of this psalm and the arrangement of it are certainly interesting. It was written with a great deal of care. It is an acrostic that is a little different from that of any other psalm. Instead of having only one verse that begins with each of the twenty-two letters of the Hebrew alphabet, there are eight verses for each letter, beginning with aleph, beth, gimel, and so on, thus resulting in 176 verses for this psalm.

As you follow the pathway through Psalm 119, you will look at only a few verses under each Hebrew letter, with a bit more focus in some areas. *Aleph* is the first letter; read verses 1 and 2. God does not want you to lose your zest for learning about Him!

Beth is the second letter; read verse 11. Hiding God's Word in your heart doesn't mean that you have to memorize it, only that you must obey it.

Gimel is the third letter; read verse 18. God's Word only becomes precious to us when we ask God Himself to reveal it to us.

In the section of the fourth letter, *daleth*, read verse 25. So many things in today's world pull us down. We gravitate in the direction of dust. Not only will our bodies fall downward, but our souls will be pulled down also by the world. God's Word has the power to revive us and lift us up.

Now read verse 33 from the *he* section, the fifth letter of the Hebrew alphabet. We want to follow on with God, run the race with patience, and look only to Jesus.

The sixth letter is *vav*; from that section, read verses 41 and 47. Does it give you joy to read the Word of God? Do you love the Bible? If not, ask God to give you a love for His Word. That is a request that God is very happy to fill!

The seventh letter is *zain*; its eight verses, 49–56, deal with the comfort of the Word. These verses have some similarity to Psalm 1. Take time to review that psalm.

Now read Psalm 119:40–56, in The Living Bible if possible.

The zain section uniquely stresses how placing our hope in God's Word brings comfort to us when we are suffering. We know that God's promises are true and that when we are afflicted, His promises can sustain us. We do not need to give in to the temptations of the ungodly, because we know what their punishment will be one day. We simply need to keep our focus on God's Word to remain on the path with Him. Our true comfort and joy come from knowing the Lord and walking with Him.

Dear Lord,

Thank You for inspiring David to write this psalm. It is a beautiful description of having faith in You. When I become distressed by all of the things going wrong in the world, help me to remember what David said in Psalm 119:13–14: "Just tell me what to do and I will do it, Lord. As long as I live I'll wholeheartedly obey. Make me walk along the right paths for I know how delightful they really are" (TLB).

Thank You for being my guide, Lord, as I follow the path with You. Amen.

On a Pathway through Some Psalms: Psalm 119 #2—Praise tothe Word of God!

As you learned in the previous lesson, Psalm 119 is the longest of all of the psalms, with 176 verses. Every verse is praise to the Word of God. One picture will not do, so Psalm 119 overflows with images from David, a man who had learned to "hope in God's Word." You learned that it is an acrostic psalm that was written with a great deal of care. There are eight verses for each of the twenty-two letters of the Hebrew alphabet, resulting in 176 verses. In this study, you will be looking again at only a few verses under each Hebrew letter.

In the previous lesson, verses stopped with the seventh letter, so this lesson will pick up at letter eight, *cheth*. Read verse 62. Have you ever thanked God in the middle of the night for His Word? Well, wake up tonight and do that!

From letter nine, *teth,* read verses 69–70. Critics of the Bible need to go on a diet, said Bible teacher and radio minister Dr. McGee, or they may die of heart trouble. We need to stay close to the Word of God. It is marvelous for heart trouble!

Read verse 73 from Hebrew letter ten, *jod.* God made us, and He always knows what we need. One of our basic needs in His Word, and that is exactly what the psalmist is talking about here.

In *caph*, letter eleven, this psalm speaks about who is persecuted but not forsaken. Read verse 83. "A bottle in the smoke" or "a wineskin in the smoke" refers to a wineskin "bottle" hung above the fire, which would become blackened, parched, and cracked. What a picture of David, who endured long and severe persecution! But he was not forsaken, because the Word of God was his stay. The same will be true for us when we cling to God's Word.

Read verse 89 from letter twelve, *lamed*. God's Word is in heaven; that's where the original copy is. Heaven and earth may pass away, but where God is, it will never pass away. And remember that the Word does not only mean what is written in the Bible; it also refers to Jesus! Read John 1:1–5 and Hebrews 13:8.

From *mem*, letter thirteen, read verses 97 and 99. The psalmist meditated on God's Word because he loved it; then he loved it even more because he had meditated upon it! A humble believer who sits at the feet of Jesus has often more skill in the Word than a person who has earned a PhD!

Letter fourteen, *nun*, includes a verse you may have often heard throughout your life and may have even memorized. Read verse 105. As you follow the pathway through God's Word, always be willing to share its light with other people.

Read verse 113 from letter fifteen, *samech*. How much time do you spend reading newspaper or magazines, compared to the time you spend reading the Bible? God is telling us, through this psalmist, that He hates vain thoughts. As you spend more time in the Word of God, you will become less and less affected by so many of the sinful events that show up in the news.

Letter sixteen is *airr*; read verse 126 from that section. This is a good prayer for us to pray today. Our prayer could be, "Lord, much of the world and much of our own country seems to have forgotten You. Help all of us who are Christians to get Your Word out to our own communities and to the world around us."

Letter seventeen, *pe,* includes verse 129. God's Word is full of wonderful revelations, commands, and promises. Even though so much of the sin in the world fills our eyes with tears (read verse 136), we are encouraged by God's Word (read verse 130).

Read verse 137 from letter eighteen, *tzaddi.* We can rest in the truth of God's righteousness, even when we question the reasons for our trials and troubles. Read also verse 143.

Are you beginning to long for a more intimate relationship with the Savior? Is your heart's cry to fall more deeply in love with Jesus? The verses based on the nineteenth letter, *koph,* are a cry of the heart for such a relationship. Read verses 145–153.

Now read verses 147–148. When is the psalmist crying to God and meditating on His Word?
Which verse from David's Psalm 1 best summarizes these verses?

How can you apply this to your own life?

Read verse 154 from the twentieth letter, *resh.* The psalmist is praying, "Redeem me according to Your Word." God's Word is the only thing that can revive us and redeem us! We need to pray for that to also occur in our own nation and all around the world!

From the twenty-first set, *schin,* read verse 161. The psalmist had more respect and awe for the Word of God than he had for the rulers of the world. I'm sure that we as Christians feel that way too!

From the final set, letter twenty-two, *tau,* read verse 176. As long as the Word of God is in your heart, as long as there is a deep longing within you to come close to God, He, the Good Shepherd, will be looking out for you. He will lift you to His shoulder and carry you back to the fold.

As you have seen from these 176 verses, Psalm 119 is a glorious psalm that glorifies the Word of God. As did the author, we need to pray for a revival of God's Word and a willingness to reflect its light to the world around us.

Dear Lord, thank You for inspiring one of Your children, so many years ago, to write such a beautiful psalm. Please encourage me to read it—and *all* of Your Word—and to continue to grow in my faith and trust in You. Thank You for the love that You show to me through Your Word and through my salvation through Your Son, Jesus. In His name I pray. Amen.

On a Pathway through Some Psalms: Psalm 150—Praise and Worship

Read Psalm 150.

What is worship? The answer is found in verse 1 of Psalm 150: "Praise the Lord." The emphasis is on the Lord; He is the object of our worship. The psalms put an emphasis upon two things: God as both the *Creator* and the *Redeemer*. God works in a field where He has no competition at all. Because of this, He demands from *all* of His creatures their worship, their adoration, and their praise.

The scriptures also tell us that God is a jealous God. Read Exodus 20:5. God created each of us for Himself, and He has redeemed each of us for Himself. Just as a husband who loves his wife does not share her with other men, so believers, called in scripture "the bride of Christ," are created solely for the Lord. Read Isaiah 62:5.

Now read Revelation 22:8–9. John, when he was on the island of Patmos, felt constrained to fall down and worship the angel who had been so helpful in bringing all of the visions before him. But God does not want His angels to be worshiped, or Mary to be worshiped, or the saints to be worshiped. Yes, they can be thanked and honored, but God wants no one to be worshiped but Himself. The Bible tells us, as in Psalm 145:10, that a day is coming when *everything* that has breath will praise the Lord!

We see that God is the object of worship, but who can actually worship and glorify Him? Read Psalm 150:6. God created the universe so that it might glorify Him. *Who* can worship, according to Job 38:7?

What will worship, according to Psalm 96:1–13a?

Humankind was also created for praise; God's great purpose is to bring humans back into the harmony of heaven. Through the giving of His own life, Jesus brought humankind back into harmony with God's tremendous creation. Today the redeemed are the ones to lift their voices in praise. Read Psalm 107:1–2.

And there is exultation in worship! This does not mean the exultation of God; rather, this is the exultation of humankind! Read Acts 9:1–6. Paul fell into the dust on the Damascus Road, and the Lord Jesus dealt with him there. But then Jesus told Paul to arise and stand on his feet. Only the Christian faith has ever lifted a man out of the dust of sinfulness and put him on his feet. Read Revelation 1:12–18. We who have been lost in sin can now come up onto our feet and worship Christ! Even as the world is filled with sin, as we await Jesus's return, we can bow before Him in adoration and praise!

Return to Psalm 150 and read it out loud as you thank God for His Word and salvation!

On a Pathway through Some Psalms Conclusion

As you have followed the pathway through some of the psalms, you have read and learned that each of us individually is a special part of God's creation; that He loves you; and that He will *always* care for you if you put your faith and trust in Him.

You have also learned that the more time you spend in prayer and praise with your heavenly Father, keeping your focus on the salvation that He has promised to give to you through His Son, Jesus, and allowing the Holy Spirit to increase your faith, the more you will be filled with joy, even as you continue to live in the sinful world.

Oh, dear Lord, it has been such a blessing to read and study Your holy Word. Thank You, Lord, for the love and salvation that You have given to me. Lord, I am so delighted to praise You with my prayers and songs of thanksgiving! As I continue to study Your Word and follow more pathways through other books of the Bible, help me to be a light of reflection of Your love and grace to other people. In the name of Your Son, Jesus, my Savior, I pray. Amen.

A Poetic Reflection Based on Bible Verses

1. Lord, I want to be a tree; Lord, I want to be a tree!
I want to send my roots way down in the ground
To where the streams of Living Water are found.
I'll be as green as I can be;
Lord, I want to be a tree! (Psalm 1:3)

2. Lord, I want to bear some fruit; yes, I want to bear some fruit!
I want my branches filled with goodness and love
And all the fruit the Spirit sends from above.
From my tip down to my root
Lord, I want to bear some fruit! (John 15:5)

3. And I want to be a light; yes, I want to be a light.
I want to send Your beam of love all around
So that a path to You can clearly be found—
A ray of hope in darkest night.
Lord, I want to be a light! (Psalm 119:105)

4. And I want to be some salt; yes, I want to be some salt.
I want to help preserve and ward off decay
And add Your pleasure to my life every day:
A recipe without a fault!
Lord, I want to be some salt! (Matthew 5:13)

5. And I want to be a lamb; yes, I want to be a lamb.
I want to cuddle up in Your loving arm
Where I'll always be protected from harm.
I know You'll love me as I am;
Lord, I want to be a lamb! (Psalm 23:1)

6. And I want to praise Your name; yes, I want to praise
Your name!
I want to thank You, Lord, for all that I am:
A tree, some fruit, a light, some salt, and a lamb.
I'll be forever glad You came!
Lord, I want to praise Your name!

Pam Talks to Parents

In the fourth section of this book, Pam talks to parents to encourage them to raise their children with a strong Christian faith. Proverbs 22:6 (RSV) tells us to "Train up a child in the way he should go, and when he is old he will not depart from it."

Whether you are a parent, a grandparent, an aunt or uncle, or someone else in charge of raising a child, you know that it can often be a challenge. But God's Word does offer help for this!

So, the fourth and final section of this book takes a look at one full year of these challenges, beginning in September, which is when the school year has fully begun, and continuing through August, month by month.

Rely on God's Word as you prepare to experience the new school year with your child(ren). God will always be with you, and He will bless you!

Trust in the Lord with all your heart, and do not rely on your own insight. In all your ways acknowledge Him, and He will make your paths straight. (Proverbs 3:5–6 RSV)

Pam Talks to Parents

"Oh, How We Need the Word!"

Throughout the world's history, many have tried
To build a society that could provide
A setting that's perfect, all needs satisfied,
Leaving envy and thievery unneeded, untried.

Why does every attempt at utopia fail?
For what reason does Shangri La not prevail?
The best of intentions are doomed from the start
Because of the evil in each human heart.

For centuries, it's been taught that people could,
If allowed to evolve, be inherently good.
But whenever you hear this—it's still being said—
Let all danger signals go off in your head!

For it's out of the heart that all evils proceed,
So having our needs met won't keep us from greed.
Even Adam and Eve, who we know had it all,
Caved into temptation, which led to their fall.

The devil, a lion, through devious ways
Effectively lures us away from God's grace.
To whom can we turn? Whose advice can we heed?
God's Word gives us all the protection we need:

The sword of the Spirit;
The strong belt of truth;
The great shield of faith (so effective from youth
To quench fiery darts that the wicked one throws);

The breastplate of righteousness God's mercy shows;
Salvation's the helmet, protecting the head;
And shoes provide swiftness as God's Word is spread.

Thus dressed, we rejoice! All our sins are forgiven!
Christ's blood has redeemed us! We're going to heaven!
Once blessed with the truth, it's our mission to share
The Good News with others, so they will be there!

The Lord's law is perfect, converting the soul,
Causing hearts that were broken to now be made whole
Through God's holy Word. Even children are given
The truths that will give them assurance of heaven.

God's grace, multifaceted, shining, and bright,
Guides us through all darkness. His Word is the light!
And parents are urged to tell each generation
The wonderful news of God's plan of salvation!

(Inspired by a sermon given by Pastor James Haberkost. Scripture references include Matthew 15:19; 1 Peter 5:8; Ephesians 6:14–17; Psalm 19:7; Psalm 119:105; and Psalm 78:5–6.)

Pam Talks to Parents: September

Hello! I hope your school year has gotten off to a happy start and that you are enjoying life with your student.

Realistically, often the start of the new school year is a depressing time of life for many parents.

So let's take a look at the subject of depression this month. Did you know that depression is experienced by the whole body? It's not only in the mind; it's a feeling of sadness or despair that's felt in the stomach as much as in the head.

According to the Bible, depression has been around for a very long time. King Saul, for example, suffered greatly from it. But the Bible is also a resource for coping with depression. When King David was depressed, God inspired him to write, in Psalms, words of comfort that we all can use.

But is depression a sin? When we feel depressed, we often don't want to read the Bible or pray. We need to recognize our own sinful, spiritual condition and seek God's forgiveness for our sins. Depression may be the *consequence* of sin. And we may need to turn to outside help—pastor, prayer partner, or doctor—to find the help we need. We mustn't allow the *feeling* of depression to keep us from dealing with the *cause* of it.

If your child is experiencing a period of depression, be available to listen, listen, listen! Resist the impulse to give advice or false cheer. Be nonjudgmental. And don't be afraid to seek outside help if you sense that your child needs it. A child in our family suffers major depression each winter due to a clinically diagnosed seasonal affective disorder. Professional counseling and the proper medication make a world of difference in that child's life!

Always remember that God understands how you feel, much better than you do! Read Psalm 69 verses 3, 29, and 30. These verses describe how we sometimes feel as we are raising our child(ren). Now read verse 33 and thank the Lord for all of His help!

Relax and rely on God to restore peace to your body and soul. He *will* help you!

Pam Talks to Parents: October

When I was a little girl, my family celebrated Halloween each year by visiting a much-anticipated haunted house.

The terror was always thrilling! I never knew which characters were fake and which were real, who would make a sudden move, or where the next fright would come from. I followed so closely with my daddy, who seemed so brave as he led the way. Mother protected me from behind, and I moved along the path like a sandwich filling, experiencing the delicious thrill of being scared half to death while knowing I was well protected by my capable, loving parents.

Recently, I came upon a verse in Psalm 63 that reminded me of those childhood experiences. Psalm 63:8 (NIV) says, "My soul clings to you; Your right hand upholds me."

What a beautiful picture of our trust in the Lord as we go through difficult and frightening paths of life. We can cling to Him, knowing that He can blaze the path while He also protects us from behind. We may be afraid, but we can trust God's protection, because He is our powerful and loving heavenly Father whose "lovingkindness is better than life" (Psalm 63:3).

Please read all of Psalm 63. Then think about its message and share it with your kids as you celebrate the spookiness of Halloween together.

Pam Talks to Parents: November

A daily time with God? You've got to be kidding! There aren't enough hours in a day as it is, much less time to be alone with God!

Many parents echo these thoughts as they juggle work, home responsibilities, and their children's schedules. Reading a morning devotion, quick table prayers, and perhaps a bedtime prayer while falling asleep may sum up your spiritual life. Yet God wants more than that from His children! He has so many blessings to give us in response to our conversations with Him, and that activity takes time—time to both speak to God and to listen to His response. As an active parent, how can you manage this?

If you're like me, there are times when your whole family is willing to leave you alone—perhaps while you're doing dishes, folding laundry, or mowing the lawn. Instead of feeling self-pity and resentment at those moments, turn them into times of real blessing by praising God and thanking Him for your dishes and food to eat, for clothing to wear, for a home to live in. Then pray for those who eat the food, wear the clothes, and live in your home.

Jesus Himself taught us about prayer, and He even gave us words to pray. Read Matthew 6:7–5. Ask the Holy Spirit to guide your conversation with God during your special moments of aloneness with Him. Read Romans 8:6–28. I have received much guidance as a parent from my heavenly Father as I have dusted a room or mopped the floor. These have been times of real blessing for me. See if it can work for you too!

Pam Talks to Parents: December

Perhaps you have observed that in most love situations, there is a circle of give and take. When you give, you receive! However, if you happen to be the parent of a preteen, this circle sometimes becomes a one-way street!

Our preteens cannot often nurture us; they have barely left the stage of being nurtured themselves. This means they are often incapable of returning the love that we give to them. This can, at times, cause parenting to be a lonely, frustrating task!

The Christmas holiday season can be an especially frustrating time as we give much of our time and finances to our children, often to a response of indifference and ingratitude. Try not to take this personally! Gratitude is the beginning of wisdom, and our children are not yet wise.

So, take the time during this busy season to *nurture yourself*. Spend time with God, listen to music, visit with a friend, enjoy a favorite hobby. Taking time for yourself will arm you against your child's youthful insensitivity.

Then open your heart to receive the gifts that God has for you, as outlined in Galatians 5:23—practical gifts of love, joy, peace, patience, kindness, goodness, faithfulness, gentleness, and self-control. These gifts from your heavenly Father are the perfect gifts for parents of preteens during the busy Christmas season!

God, our perfect parent, knows exactly what we need. Read Matthew 7:11. And don't forget to say, "Thank You!"

Pam Talks to Parents: January

Two happy families, one visiting from out of state, pile into the van for the six-mile ride home from church. Chattering happily, no one notices that the three-year-old child has been left behind!

A bus pulls into a very crowded bus stop. Most of the people board the bus. When it pulls away, a young mother discovers that her toddler boarded the bus with the crowd!

A young father places his newborn child, strapped into a carrier, atop the van, while he then reaches in and buckles in the older children. Returning to the driver's side, he buckles himself in and drives away, forgetting about the new infant on top of the van!

These true stories are parents' nightmares. It is an indescribable feeling of horror to lose a child! And have you ever been the child who was lost? That feeling of terror is unforgettable as well!

We have just come through the Christmas season, in which we have again adored God's infant Son, Jesus, and have basked in the wonders of His love. The Bible assures us that God *is* love. But we are also told that God is equally a judge who cannot tolerate sin.

Over and over, God declares that one day His patience will wear out, punishment will be swift and complete, and the world as we know it will come to an end.

What if God, our heavenly Father, loses one of *us*?

In Amos 9:9, God compares the punishment of a nation to a grain that is sifted in a sieve, and He promises that "not one true kernel will be lost" (TLB). Every one of us who truly believes that Jesus, the baby of Christmas, *is* the Savior, the victor over Satan, sin, and death, a "good kernel" in God's eyes. He knows each of us by name and *never* loses track of us! Jesus said, as recorded in Matthew 19:14, "Let the children come to Me, and do not hinder them; for to such belongs the kingdom of heaven." The Bible also promises, in Mark 16:16, that "he who believes and is baptized *will* be saved."

What a wonderful promise for the new year!

Pam Talks to Parents: February

Excuse me, please.

Are you teaching your children good manners?

In this age of dinners eaten on TV tables, or of fast food grabbed on the run, the teaching of mealtime manners is often overlooked.

Showing respect for one's elders by rising when they first enter the room, the etiquette of proper introductions and manners, all seem to have gone the way of old- time telephones!

Why should we even care if our children have respectable manners? Because as Christians, we are to behave as children of the King! Good manners convey respect for one's self and for others.

If your family is slipping up in the manners department, it's not too late to make amends. In a family meeting, and in the spirit of fun and adventure, set out some guidelines for improved manners within the family. Check out a library book or two on the subject, or look on your computer or smartphone to give you some ideas.

Using good manners within your family will add a sense of dignity to your relationships. The respect practiced within the family will begin to spread to other relationships as well. Philippians 2:3 (NIV) tells us to "do nothing out of selfish ambition or vain conceit, but in humility consider others better than yourselves."

With God's help, your family can be transformed for a lifetime by this project. It's worth the effort. Try it! You'll like it!

Pam Talks to Parents: March

There are many occurrences that cause an *ouch* to enter our lives. A stubbed toe or a paper cut gives us a temporary or physical ouch. A car accident might cause an ouch with serious, long-lasting results.

An unkind word from a friend may wound us with a temporary emotional ouch, while the death of a friend causes more serious, long-lasting pain.

A small sin, such as a little white lie or deciding not to attend church one Sunday, might cause a temporary ouch in our relationship with God. Deliberately breaking a commandment, committing a crime, or falling away from worship altogether causes enormous spiritual wounds.

Although we are adults, as God's children, we experience the worst of our pain when it is spiritual. We know the rules of our Father's house, but we break them every day, whether intentionally or not, and then our relationship with our Father God feels severed by a tremendous ouch.

When God put the cross in front of the *ouch*, it became touch. God's love, through Jesus, touches our bodies with physical healing and touches our wounded spirits with restored emotional health. But most importantly, God's love through Jesus always reaches out to us with forgiveness for any sin, no matter how big or small we may feel that it is. *All* sin severs our relationship with God. That hurts Him so much! The moment we turn to our Father in repentance, He rushes toward us to welcome us back with the healing touch of love and forgiveness. When we do the same for our own children, we are teaching them about the heavenly

Father's love. Should we do any less for our own children than our Father does for us?

One of our sons recently turned twenty. As I think about his childhood, I don't find myself asking whether I sent him to camp often enough or involved him in enough other activities. Instead I wonder, *Did I hug enough? Did I listen enough? Did I forgive enough? Did I love enough?*

> Children, obey your parents; this is the right thing to do because God has placed them in authority over you. Honor your father and mother. This is the first of God's ten commandments that ends with a promise. And this is the promise: that if you honor your father and mother, yours will be a long life, full of blessings. And now a word to you parents: Don't keep on scolding and nagging your children, making them angry and resentful. Rather, bring them up with the loving discipline the Lord Himself approves, with suggestions and godly advice. (Ephesians 6:1–4 TLB)

Yes, we are imperfect parents, but God is also *our* perfect Father!

Pam Talks to Parents: April

Does your growing child's smile have a silver sparkle? Do you have one of his or her baby teeth tucked away in the corner of a dresser or a jewelry box? My children have long outgrown the days of loose teeth and braces. My second-grade piano students, however, flash me gapped-toothed smiles, and junior highers' smiles often glint with silver.

We hardly give it a thought that at about age seven, our child(ren)'s baby teeth will begin to fall out, and adult teeth take their place. It's an expected part of life. Do you know any adult with a mouth full of baby teeth?

When the orthodontist affixes braces to our child(ren)'s teeth, we believe that the teeth will respond and be coaxed into more attractive positions. That's how it works; we trust the outcome.

God created the world to be a place of order. Even though tainted by sin, the world still reflects that order, and we rely on it. We expect the sun to rise, seasons to progress, children to grow. At times, chaos seems to reign, disease or some other disaster may interrupt our flow of life, but the expected order remains as a foundation of our lives.

This is such a blessing from God! It shows us that we can totally count on His promises. His Word is truth. He will never leave us or forsake us. He will be with us always, to the end of the age. If we believe that His Son, Jesus, paid for our sins, we will live with Him forever! (Read John 17:17, Joshua 1:5, Matthew 28:20, and John 3:16.)

That's how God works. We can trust the outcome!

Pam Talks to Parents: May

Are you a smartphone-, laptop-, and computer-literate parent (or grandparent)? Oh—what? You're not? Your children seem to know more than you do?

A truth that we parents and grandparents learned in school is that every positive has a negative. The unfortunate aspect of global computer, laptop and Facebook communication is the instant access to vivid, graphic pornography, involving ever-conceivable depravity. Satan is very interested in capturing the hearts and minds of our computer-age children, and he doesn't miss a trick!

While everyone is in agreement that our children *must* be protected from these available images, the debate rages about how this should be accomplished: through government regulation and prosecution or more immediate parental intervention. The sad truth is that while the debate goes on, our children are becoming more adept at the computer, smartphone, and laptop and even more curious about these forbidden images.

We cannot turn to parents of previous generations for help with this issue. Our wisdom can come only from God Himself. So, parents and grandparents, I urge you to *pray* and to *keep the lines of communication open* with your kids. Encourage them to talk to you about all the things they see and hear. *Don't react*. Don't become offended or angry. Simply *listen* to your kids, and if they ask you questions, answer them honestly. Point them to God's Word for guidance and forgiveness.

And if you feel that your own life is not such a hot example of Christian living, ask God for forgiveness and help. He loves to answer prayers like this! God, who created your kids and loves them even more than you do, wants them to enjoy every blessing of the world they live in, including all the good things that computers, laptops, and smartphones have to offer.

"Be strong in the Lord and in the strength of His might. Put on the whole armor of God, that you may be able to stand against the wiles of the devil" (Ephesians 6:10–11RSV).

You have instant access to the God of the universe. He is never *down*, and you don't have to know a thing about today's technology to reach Him!

Pam Talks to Parents: June

Another school year has ended! Under summer skies, we can enjoy a season that is less frantic and even relaxing. But as you enjoy the time of vacation from the school-year pace, don't take a vacation from God!

When I was growing up, if our family went away for a weekend or even two weeks, whether we visited relatives or friends or visited a distant state, we always found a church to attend on Sunday morning. It was fun to compare orders of service, hear hymns sung in different regional accents, and feel the kinship of the body of Christ in a place far from home.

The example that my parents set was not lost on my brother, sister, or me. God commands that we set aside one day each week to worship Him. Because we love the Lord, but more importantly, because He loves us, we desire to obey Him. The experience of worship is a joy, not a burden; it is an activity we relish, not an interruption to our lives.

If you have never visited a church while traveling with our family, why not give it a try this summer? It may turn out to be a high point of your vacation!

O come, let us sing to the Lord;
Let us make a joyful noise to the Rock of our salvation!
Let us come into His presence with thanksgiving,
Let us make a joyful noise to Him with songs of praise!

O come, let us worship and bow down;
Let us kneel before the Lord our Maker!
(Psalm 95:1–2, 6 RSV)

Pam Talks to Parents: July

One of the difficulties of parenting kids in junior high is that, although they need parents' closeness, love, and discipline as much as ever, they are becoming independent and wish to test the waters of separation. Especially in the summer, moments of family togetherness that used to be so cozy and pleasant suddenly bloom into times of tension and discord. This is so distressing for the entire family! What can be done about it?

It helps to consider family activities that can allow the young person to include a friend and then offer them a bit of independence within the framework of the activity. With some creative planning and a family review of any rules, summer activities can still be happy times for everyone. For example, if the whole family is going to a movie, let your junior higher sit with another one of your children or a friend in a different part of the theater. It's OK! Afterward, you can all meet up to continue with further plans.

Plan vacation days that allow your young people to be on their own yet within a defined area (such as a theme part or a water park) and with specific check-in time. ("OK, have fun. Check in with us at the food court between one and one thirty.") These experiences begin to allow our children to separate from us as parents. Remember, that *is* our ultimate goal in raising children!

If you plan a longer vacation, let your young person aid in the planning. I was thrilled when our family took a side trip to a historical mining town during a vacation in Colorado, due to my excited suggestion. I felt valued by my parents, who respected my teenage sense of adventure.

Include a friend whenever possible. Friendships are *extremely* important to young people. This doesn't mean that the family bonds are diminishing; rather, they can be strengthened when our children see that we respect who they are.

First Timothy 4:7 and 12 (TLB) tell us this: "Don't waste time arguing over foolish ideas and silly myths and legends. Spend your time and energy in the exercise of keeping spiritually fit … Don't let anyone think little of you because you are young. Be their ideal; let them follow the way you teach and live; be a pattern for them in your love, your faith, and your clean thoughts."

God bless your family with a happy summer!

Pam Talks to Parents: August

August is a special time when you are raising a family. It's still summer, but the evenings aren't quite as long or late. In addition, the excitement of a new school year begins to color plans that are made.

If your child is entering junior high, that excitement may also be mixed with apprehension. New teachers, perhaps a new school building, and undoubtedly new classmates add an element of the unknown. Your junior higher's own physical and emotional changes may also add to the unknown!

So often, junior high kids are downright irritating to be around. Wills clash; nitpicking leads to full-scale arguments. Yet, parents, these are the most crucial years to learn to listen, to not become angry, and to keep the lines of communication open. Our heavenly Father (who could often become impatient with us!) gives this advice in James 1:19 (NIV): "Be quick to listen, slow to speak, and slow to become angry."

(I find that the whole book of James offers wonderful instructions for parents. It's a short, practical book. Take a look at it!)

August is also a perfect time to establish some of the school routines to be followed *as a family*. Be sure that all the components of Christian growth are in your plans. Regular Sunday worship, Bible study, and church youth activities are all designed to help your junior higher grow and develop both socially and spiritually. Encourage your preteen to take full advantage of these activities! And let them be a reflection of good Christian growth to any younger children that you may have or with whom they frequently associate.

Finally, parents, "If any of you lacks wisdom, he should ask God, Who gives generously to all without finding fault, and it will be given to him" (James 1:5 NIV).

God bless you and your family as the new school year begins!

I thank You, my Heavenly Father, through Jesus Christ, Your dear Son, that You have kept me this night from all harm and danger, and I pray that You would keep me this day also from sin and every evil, that all my doings and life may please You. For into Your hands I commend myself, my body and soul, and all things. Let Your holy angel be with me, that the evil foe may have no power over me. Amen.

(From Martin Luther's *Small Catechism*)

Heavenly Father, send Your Holy Spirit into our hearts to direct and rule us according to Your will, to comfort us in all our afflictions, to defend us from all error, and to lead us into all truth, through Jesus Christ, our Lord. Amen.

Cast all your cares on the Lord and He will sustain you! (Psalm 55:22 NIV)

Some Concluding Thoughts on The Gift of God's Word

The Bible includes quite a few verses that speak about gifts. God's Word is a wonderful gift to us because it teaches us about God's love for us and His plan for our eternal salvation. So it is very important that we read God's Word and ask Him to guide us with understanding of what He is teaching us.

Here are some wonderful verses in The Living Bible translations:

For the wages of sin is death; but the free gift of God is eternal life through Jesus Christ our Lord. (Romans 6:23)

Because of His kindness you have been saved through trusting Christ. And even trusting is not of yourselves; it too is a gift from God. Salvation is not a reward for the good we have done, so none of us can take any credit for it. It is God Himself Who has made us what we are and given us new lives from Christ Jesus. (Ephesians 2:8–9)

And if you hardhearted, sinful men know how to give good gifts to your children, won't your Father in heaven even more certainly give good gifts to those who ask Him for them? (Matthew 7:11)

But whatever is good and perfect comes to us from God, the Creator of all light, and He shines forever without change or shadow. And it was a happy day for Him when He gave us our new lives, through the truth of His Word, and we became, as it were, the first children of His new family. (James 1:17–18)

Thank God for His Son—His Gift too wonderful for words! (2 Corinthians 9:15)